Brian's List

Brian's List

26 ½ easy to use ideas on how to live a fun, balanced, healthy life

BY G. BRIAN BENSON
ILLUSTRATED BY PAUL HERNANDEZ

REAWAKEN MEDIA
LOS ANGELES, CA

Reawaken Media
Los Angeles, CA
www.gbrianbenson.com

© 2009 by G. Brian Benson
All rights reserved.
First edition published 2009. Second edition 2018.
No part of this book may be reproduced or transmitted in any form or by any means, electronic or mechanical, including photocopying, recording, or by any information storage retrieval system, without permission in writing from the publisher.

Printed in the United States of America

ISBN: 978-0-9822286-2-3

Cover design by Davon Embler
Illustrations by Paul Hernandez
Front cover, back cover and inside cover author photos by Jenny Felimi Photography, Los Angeles, CA

To my son Michael.
May you be happy, weightless
and in love with the world!

We Are Meant To Succeed

Have you ever felt whiny, angry or sad?
Or tired and frustrated and then acted mad?
You're not alone, we've all been there before
When we're all out of sorts and acted quite poor

Take heart and take heed, it's the balance of life
Some days we're quite happy, others feeling some strife
The key to this game, is to understand how it's played
When you know what to expect, your confusion will fade

Love flows in balance, it's where we should be
Not too high, not too low, but the middle, you see
Be thankful and happy for where you are at
Life here's for learning, it's as simple as that

So during those times when it's tough or unsure
Take a step back and think thoughts good or pure
Remember a time when you had some success
Believe in yourself and never ever second guess

Your life is perfection, the good times and bad
The easy and the tough, the happy and the sad
Each challenge brings a chance to grow and become whole
To learn from mistakes, and reconnect with your soul

We are meant to succeed, so take heart and take flight
Throw out your fears and give way to love's light
Your destiny beckons, your true nature's at hand
Live life to its fullest, it's fantastic and grand!

G. Brian Benson
10-24-07

Be who you are and say what you feel, because those who mind don't matter and those who matter don't mind.

—Dr. Seuss

Contents

	Treasure Map	11
	Welcome	13
-1-	Take a moment for yourself	15
-2-	Have an open mind	19
-3-	Clean house	23
-4-	Make amends	27
-5-	Drink more water	31
-6-	Give thanks	35
-7-	Go for a walk	39
-8-	Listen to music	41
-9-	Clear out any unwanted or unused items	45
-10-	Read a book	49
-11-	Watch an inspirational show or movie	53
-12-	Treat yourself with respect	57
-13-	Get more sleep	61
-14-	Go exercise	65
-15-	Write down your thoughts	69
-16-	Hang out with positive people	73
-17-	Set a goal and follow through with it	77
-18-	Try something new, take a chance	81
-19-	Give	85

–20–	Meditate	89
–21–	Listen to your heart	93
–22–	Do what you love	97
–23–	Live in the moment—be present	101
–24–	Eat better, eat less	105
–25–	Leave 10 minutes early	109
–26–	Laugh	113
–26½–	Other ideas to help you stay balanced	117

Final thought	121
Believing eyes	123
Acknowledgements	124
Other works	127
About Brian	129

Treasure Map

In search of treasure, we look for a map
A guide to riches fulfilled.
An outline to lead us, a smooth road to travel
A sketch for happiness to yield.

We search high to the heavens and low to the earth
For reasons to quiet our mind.
We look near to friends and far to religion
For explanations and answers to find.

Our path can be difficult and filled with much pain
As we seek away from our heart.
A route void of aim, light or guidance
And back to the beginning we start.

So we gather our strength and give try again
And begin to roll with the tide.
The treasure we seek isn't high, low, near or far
But in us, resting gently inside.

Copyright G. Brian Benson 2011

Welcome

The idea for this book came about from a piece of paper that I carried around in my backpack titled "Things that keep me balanced and on the right path." It was a list of things that I compiled that kept me centered and in the flow. Whenever I was out of balance I would refer to this list and begin to utilize some of its cues. Most of the cues in this book were on my list. Some may already be a part of your life and seem familiar. Fantastic! Keep them going. Some might be new and I invite you to integrate them into your life. I realize some of these might be a stretch for you, but if you take to heart these suggestions that I am offering, there is no way your life can't improve. My wish is for you to find balance and happiness every single day for the rest of your life. Life was not meant to be a struggle. Our true nature is one of happiness, empowerment and love. Regain your true nature! Enjoy life!

Sincerely,
Brian

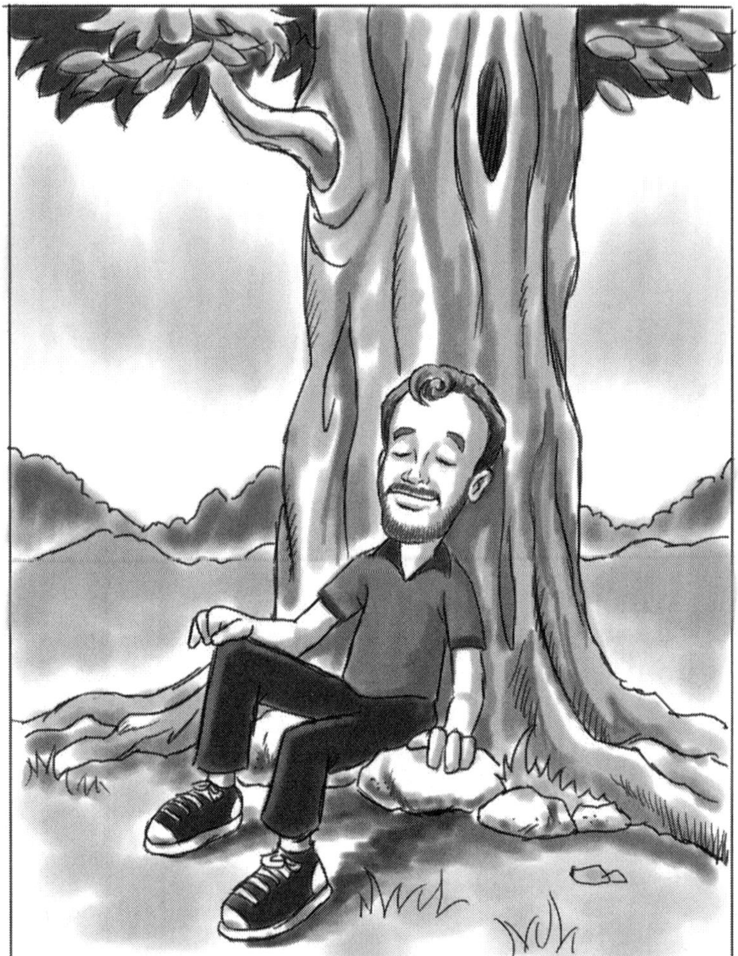

–1–

Take a moment for yourself

Do not lose your inward peace for anything whatsoever, even if your whole world seems upset.
—Saint Francis De Sales

With today's world becoming busier and busier, it's no wonder that people are having many more stress-related health problems. If you think about it, with all the technology at our fingertips it has become much harder to escape from work, other obligations and all those people who may want to try to track you down. With cell phones, social media, email and text messages it can sometimes feel overwhelming to get a moment's respite to get centered and regain your bearings.

However allowing yourself a few minutes here and there to take a deep breath and relax can and will make all the difference and keep you energized throughout the day. Take a short walk, sit down in a park, and eat lunch in silence. If you can't get away from people or your place of work, sneak out to your car and close your eyes. Take some deep breaths to regain your balance. You may have to get creative to create some space for yourself, but it will be well worth it!

What could you do to take a moment for yourself?

1)

2)

3)

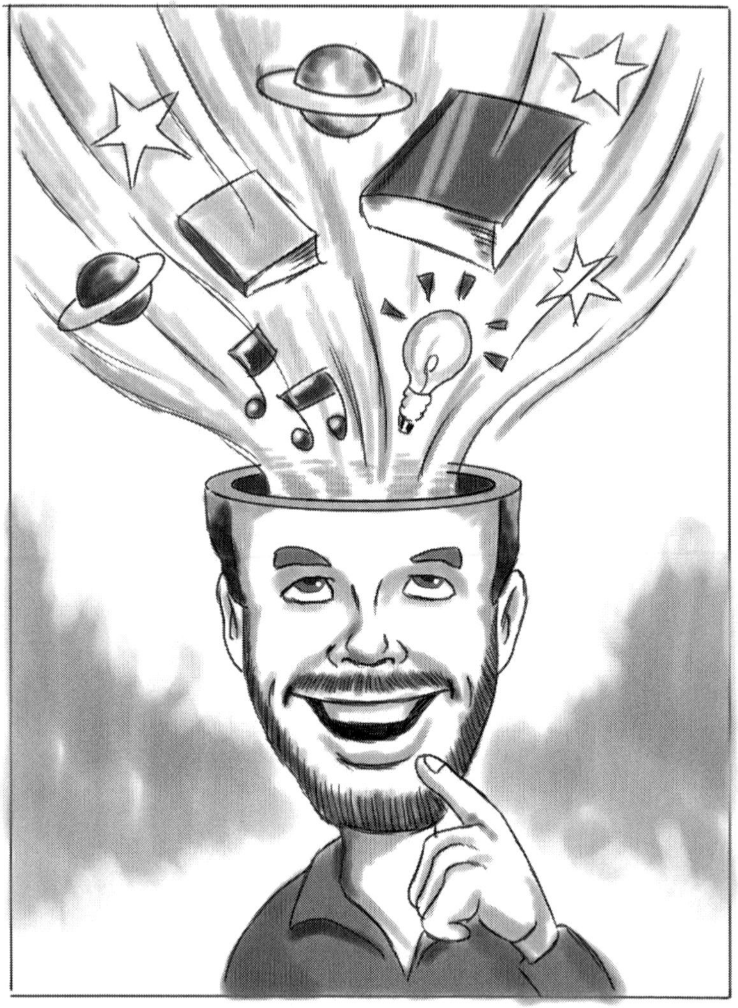

–2–

Have an open mind

The real act of discovery consists not in finding new lands, but in seeing with new eyes.
—Marcel Proust

This is one of those things that took me a while to figure out. Not that I thought that I had all of the answers, just that sometimes I would play devil's advocate rather quickly on ideas that were presented to me. Instead of hearing something out, I would immediately begin to say why a particular idea wouldn't work. I have since come to realize that there are a couple of reasons to keep an open mind and be open to whatever comes your way.

First and foremost is that it might be a better way of doing things! You just never know. I can guarantee you that anyone who has ever been successful at anything realizes that he or she doesn't have all of the answers. And they certainly have been open to suggestions on new ways of doing things along their path to success.

The second reason is that it makes you a better listener. This is a lesson that most of us can use some help on. People appreciate being heard. The more you let other people speak, the more it empowers them. "How does this help me?" you ask. Well, it might provide you with some great ideas or new ways to look at things, but it will also strengthen the bond between you and the person you are talking with. Whether it's a co-worker, your best friend or a family member, it doesn't matter. It will allow them to feel heard and like they are part of the conversation.

You can't help but not benefit by having an open mind. It will make you a better person!

Are you open to other people's ideas?

Do you consider yourself a good listener?

How could you improve?

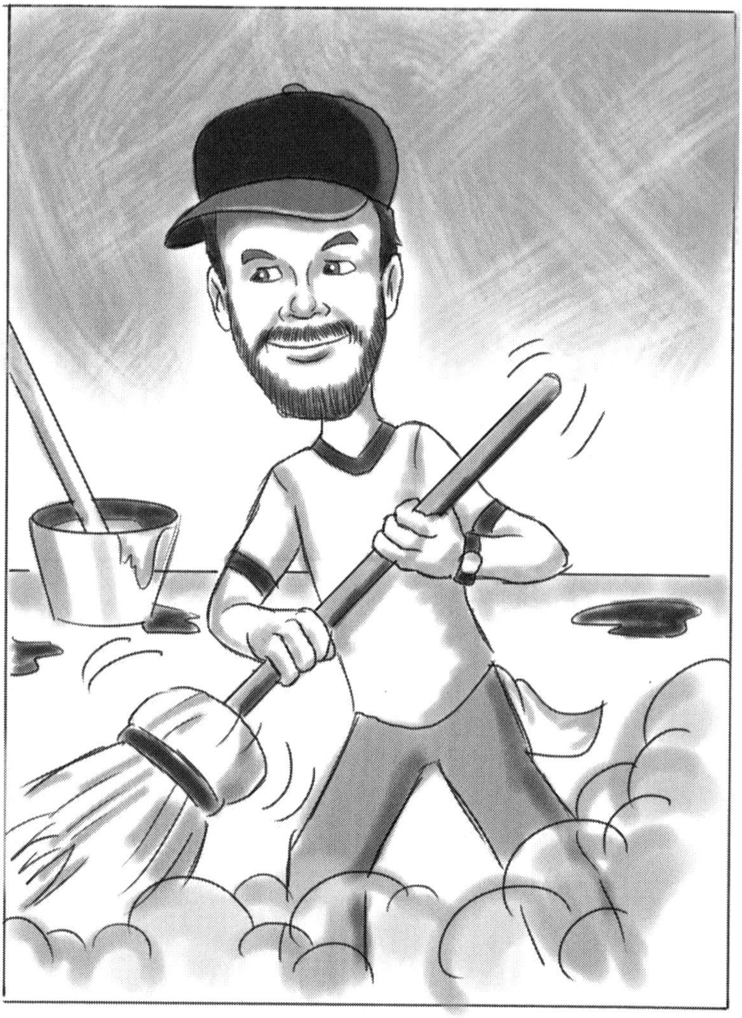

−3−

Clean house

Cleanliness is next to Godliness.
—JOHN WESLEY

How do you feel when you get home from work and notice that your house or apartment is dirty or out of sorts? It isn't a nice feeling, is it? It feels very heavy, almost like there is a large weight just resting on your shoulders. Let's get rid of that burdensome feeling by tidying up and cleaning house. What might originally take only a couple of hours will make a huge difference in your attitude and, more importantly, will free up your mind and let you truly relax, ahhhh . . . And better yet, after your initial cleaning, tidying up and keeping your place in order is not only easier and less time-consuming, but an empowering feeling simply because it then takes so little to get that "fresh" feeling in your living space!

You owe it to yourself. Our homes are where we are supposed to be able to retreat to be at peace. Let your body, mind and soul rest easy. Clean house and release the heaviness!

Would your living space be considered clean?

Where are some areas that could be improved?

How would that make you feel if they were clean?

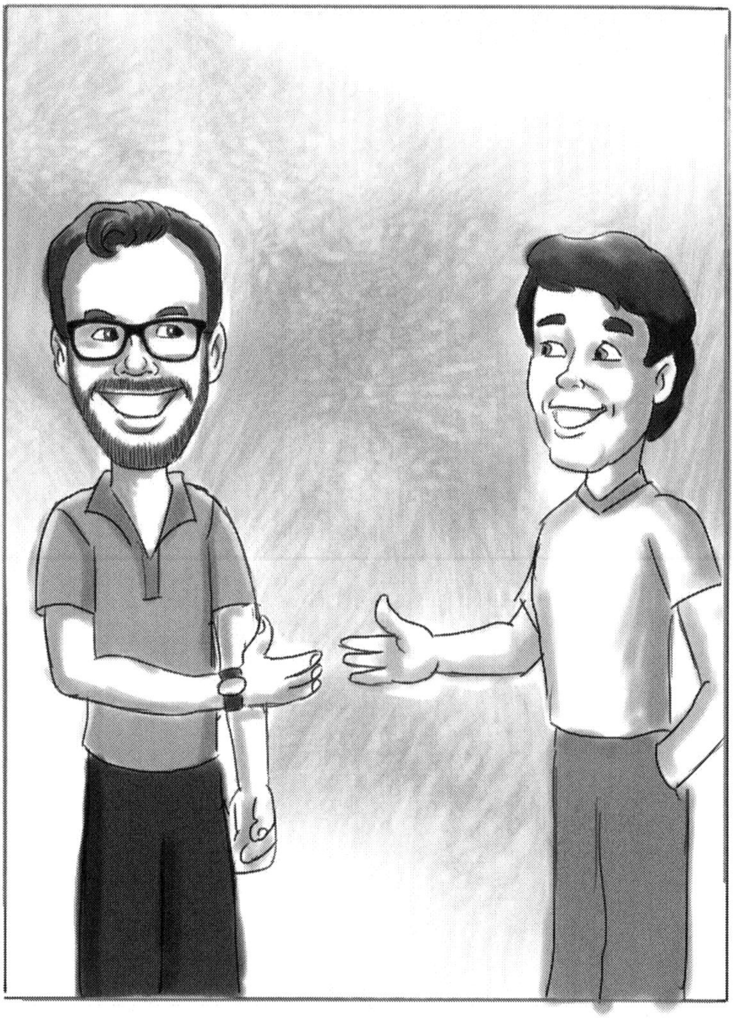

–4–

Make amends

The way we communicate with others and with ourselves ultimately determines the quality of our lives.
—Anthony Robbins

"To err is human, to forgive is divine." Ah, the wise words of Alexander Pope. Do you have any unresolved issues hanging over you? A misunderstanding with a family member, or an argument with a co-worker? We all have at one time or another. To really free ourselves of this pain, anger, guilt or confusion that we are holding onto, we need to make amends by trying to clear things up. This is so important for our mental, emotional and physical well being! It will be like a load of bricks being removed from your shoulders. You will feel yourself become lighter and you will wonder why you didn't try to make amends earlier. You know what else? It will more than likely deepen the bond that existed between yourself and the person that the misunderstanding took place with as well. Or at the very least you can agree to disagree and move on and start feeling like yourself and being productive again.

I realize that there are all kinds of problems and misunderstandings. Some problems are much bigger than others. And some misunderstandings will not be as easily rectified as others. Some require outside help such as a therapist or a trusted friend. However, each situation resolved, no matter how small, is one more step towards freedom! Give it a try! Free yourself. It doesn't matter who or what started the misunderstanding. Try to patch things up. You will live a healthier life!

Are there any people or areas in your life that you could make amends with?

1)

2)

3)

How about yourself? Is there anything you can make amends with or forgive yourself for?

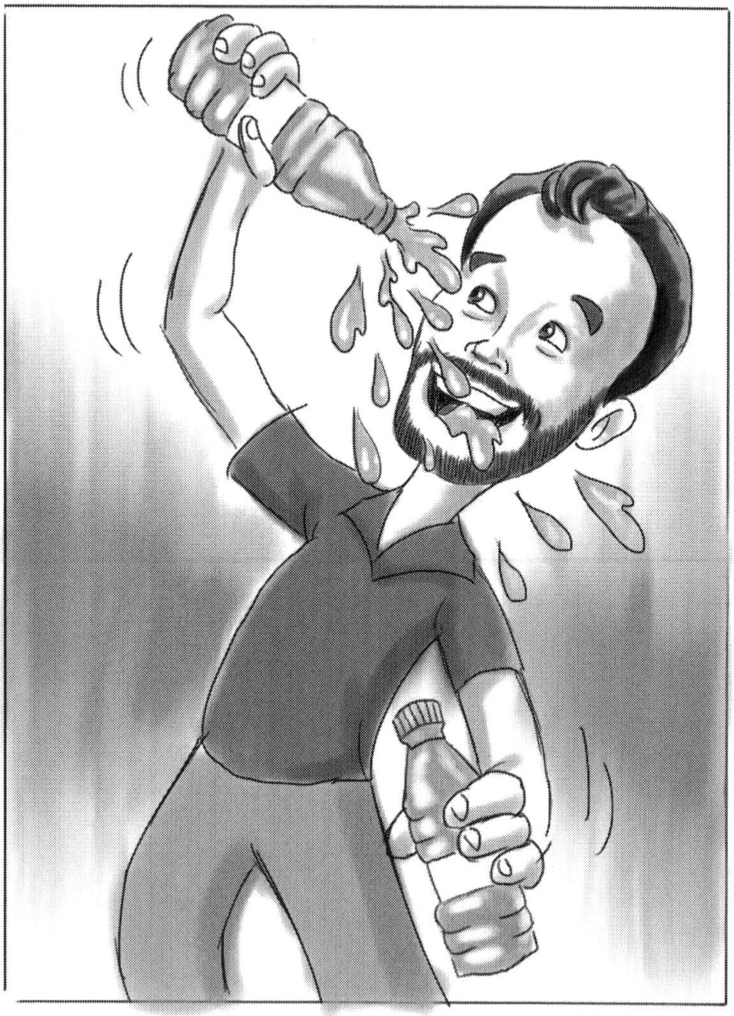

–5–

Drink more water

To understand water is to understand the cosmos, the marvels of nature and life itself.
—Masaru Emoto

Did you know that 60% of our bodies and 75% of our muscles are made up of water? Is it any wonder that a lot of people get headaches or feel fatigued when they are under-hydrated! Did you know that it has been proven that drinking enough water helps many medical conditions? Chronic fatigue, allergies, digestive problems, urinary tract problems and constipation, just to name a few. Did you know that water acts as a natural appetite suppressant and may help in weight loss? Some other benefits of drinking more water include healthier skin, better nutrient absorption and regulation of body temperature during exercise.

I know you have heard this a million times before, but if you want your body to feel and operate better, you need to drink more water! Water not only provides us with invaluable life sustenance, but it also helps us flush out our systems. Which in turn will allow our bodies to run more efficiently and provide us with more energy.

Try having 8 glasses (8 oz. each time) of water a day. Two before breakfast, two between breakfast and lunch, two between lunch and dinner and two after dinner. Being properly hydrated is well worth the trouble of having to make a couple of extra pit stops during the day. Look out—you might start feeling better!

Are you drinking enough water throughout the day?

How could you do a better job?

Some ways to support proper hydration

1) Keep a jug of water in your car.

2) Carry a reusable bottle of water with you at all times.

3) Keep a glass of water at your bedside.

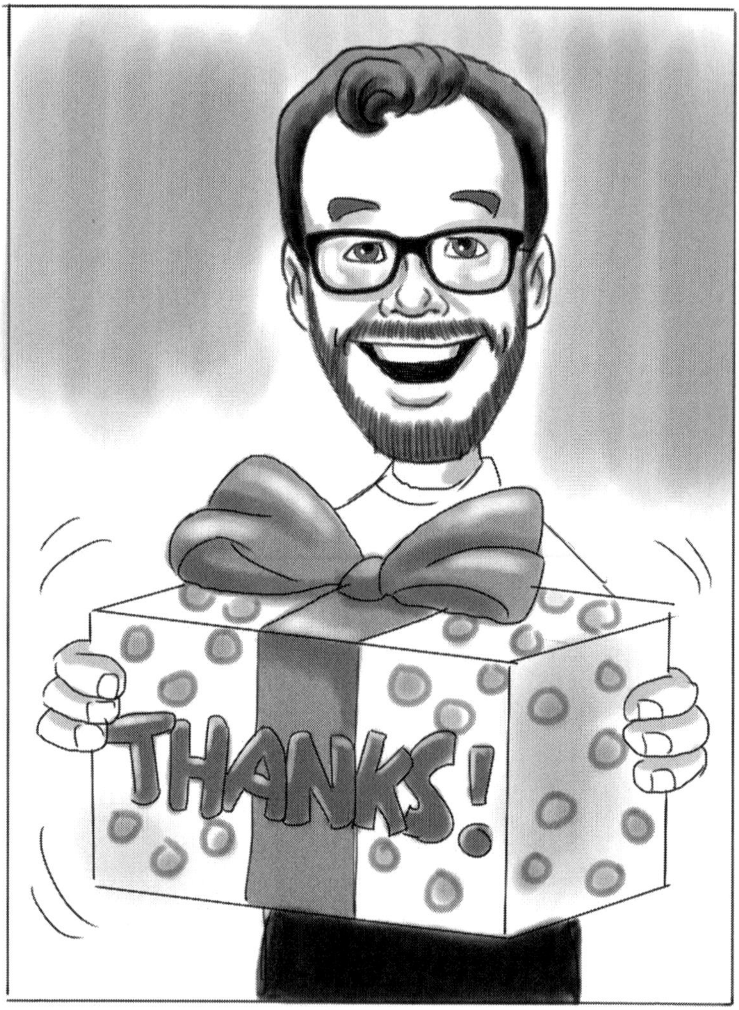
THANKS!

-6-

Give thanks

*Of all the attitudes that we can acquire,
surely the attitude of gratitude is by far the most important
and by far the most life-changing.*
—Zig Ziglar

I would like you to close your eyes and take a deep breath. As you let out your breath slowly I want you to think about all of the things in your life that you could be thankful for. It can be anything big or small. Your family, your home, your job, your car, the food that you eat, your bicycle, the country you live in, time spent with your friends, your favorite pair of shoes, and the flowers in your garden are all great examples. Giving thanks for what we have is probably the single most important thing that we can do for ourselves. It puts us in a positive frame of mind and lets the Universe know that we are open to receiving more.

I realize that there are some people that might say that they don't have a lot to be thankful for. That is understandable considering what might be going on in their life at the present moment. However, I believe everyone does have things that are blessings in their lives. And it is very important to tap into what we are thankful for to create some momentum to continue creating more things that we can give thanks about. Thoughts are things and if one doesn't feel that they have much to be grateful for, then that will become their reality because they are telling themselves that they aren't worthy. We are all worthy!

Give thanks for all that comes your way! The good and the bad. "Why would I want to give thanks for something bad that happened?" Because we are here to learn and the greatest learning opportunities usually occur during trying experiences. Be thankful for them and the new and smarter you that came out of a tough situation. They will pass, and you will be the better for it.

But most importantly, giving thanks on a regular basis will transform your attitude and allow a more positive flow into your life! Attitude is everything!

What are you thankful for?

1)

2)

3)

4)

5)

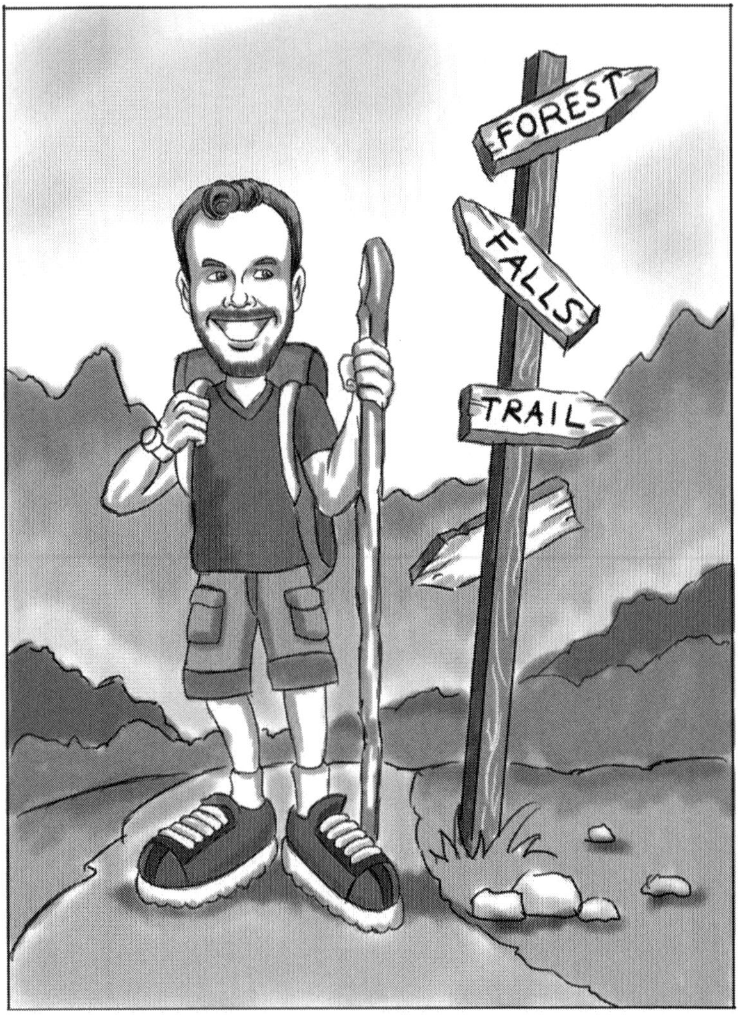
FOREST
FALLS
TRAIL

–7–

Go for a walk

*In every walk with nature
one receives far more than he seeks.*
—John Muir

Want to get your head clear about something? Want to re-connect with yourself? Want to get your creative juices flowing? Want to change your attitude? Want to give your body a little exercise? Want to get in touch with nature? Want to relieve some stress? Want to connect with a friend?

Go take a walk! It is such a powerful cure-all and . . . it is free! I can't tell you how many times I have gone for a walk and just felt totally rejuvenated during and after it. It's a fantastic way to get unstuck and wake your senses back up!

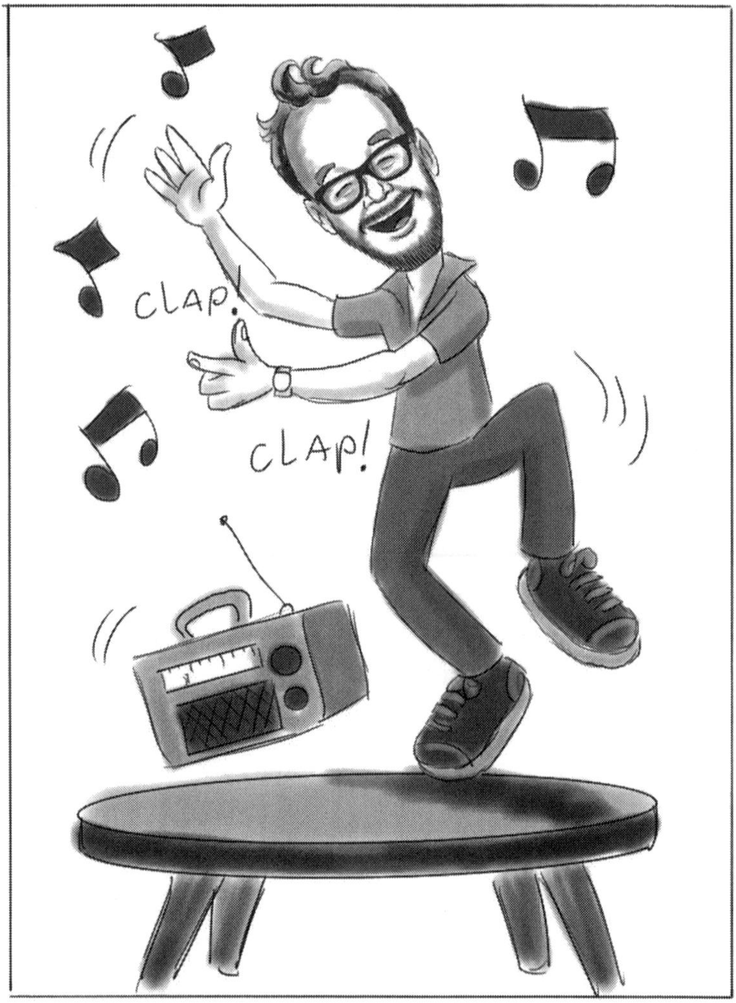
CLAP!
CLAP!

–8–

Listen to music

*Music expresses that which cannot be put into words
and that which cannot remain silent.*
—Victor Hugo

Another great way to change your attitude and give yourself a pick me up is by listening to music that inspires you. Whether it's the theme from Rocky, some easy jazz, or a nice soothing classical piece by Bach, it doesn't really matter. Just as long as it makes you feel good and feeds your soul. There is so much wonderful music out there! With all of the music streaming services like Pandora and Spotify and the online music store iTunes, it's like we can magically snap our fingers and listen to any song, band, or genre that suits our mood 24 hours a day from the comfort of our computer or cell phone. It's amazing how far music and the way we listen to it has come.

So sit back, grab a cup of tea and immerse yourself in a soulful journey listening to what makes you happy! Or if you are feeling active, put in your earbuds and listen to your iPod music on your phone while exercising at the gym or walking at the park. It is very easy to get lost in music. And sometimes that is just what the doctor ordered!

What are some of your favorite music styles or music groups that make you feel better?

1)

2)

3)

4)

5)

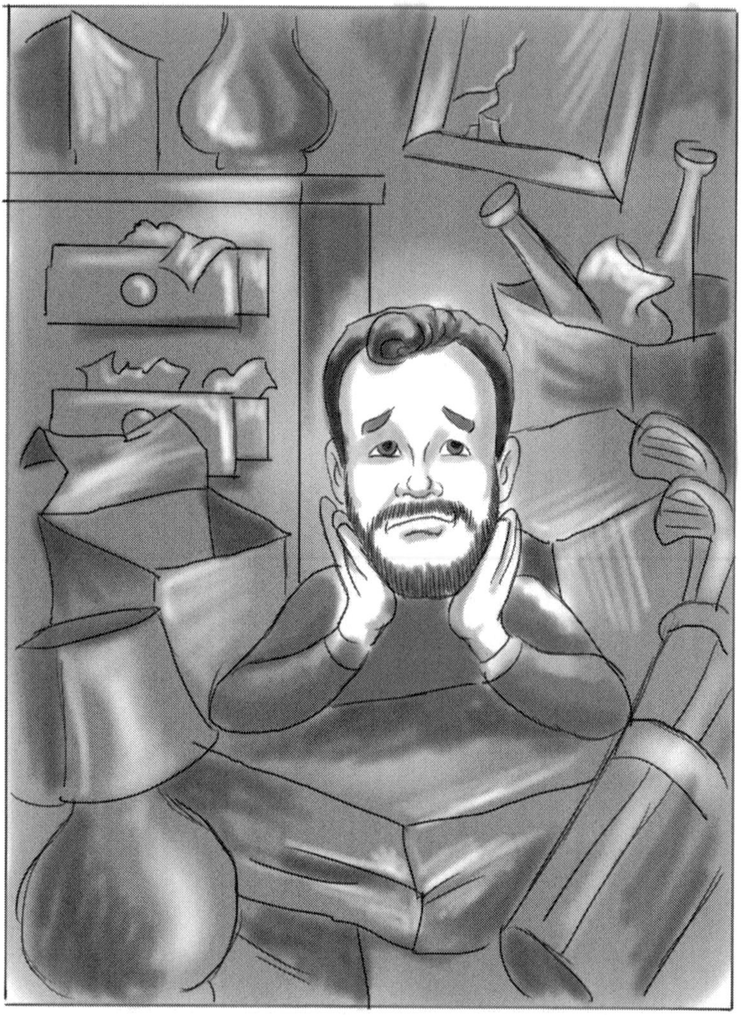

–9–

Clear out any unwanted or unused items

*It's easier traveling the road of life
when I don't have so much to carry on my back.*
—SILAS WEIR MITCHELL

Do you have anything just sitting around collecting dust? Is your garage as tidy as you would like it? Probably not. So do something about it! Get rid of any of your unused or unwanted items lying around the house. There are lots of ways to make them disappear. Donate them to a local charity, give them away to friends, or sell them.

Stuff has a way of creeping into our lives and before we know it, starts to take over! Unfinished projects are like taunting specters grabbing a hold of our sanity. Most end up clinging to—and strangling—our energy every time we see them. I feel it is much better to free ourselves of these unfinished projects and open up the space in our homes. This may allow us to regain the energy in ourselves that we were struggling to maintain. And with our reclaimed centeredness we can put to use our energy to complete the projects we truly want in our lives. Not waste it on worry about what we need to do or feel like we should do.

Feel the weight of a burden lifted as you clear out your unwanted items! Feeling light and free is a wonderful way to go through life!

Room checklist for potential clutter removal.

- ❑ Living Room
- ❑ Bedroom
- ❑ Closets
- ❑ Bathroom
- ❑ Kitchen
- ❑ Hallway
- ❑ Dining Room
- ❑ Garage
- ❑ Backyard
- ❑ Storage Unit

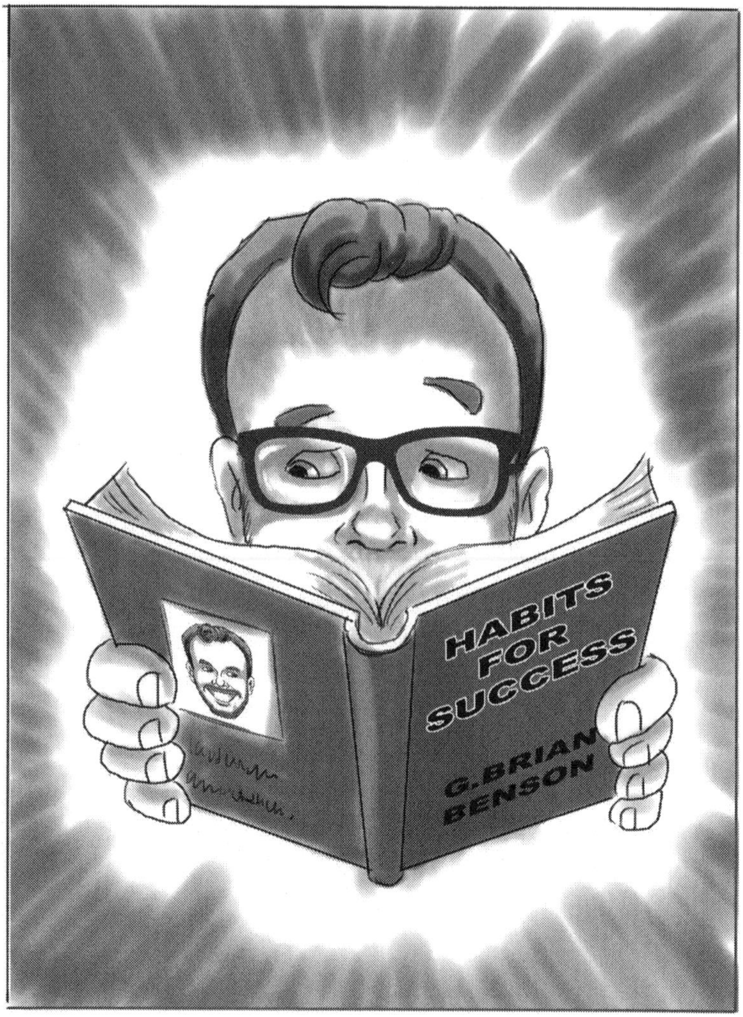
HABITS
FOR
SUCCESS
G.BRIAN
BENSON

–10–

Read a book

A library is a hospital for the mind.
—Anonymous

Get lost in a story! What a wonderful way to let your mind take a rest from a busy day or your busy schedule. I like to read at the end of the day. It's a great way to refresh my system and calm my nerves before bedtime. Any time of the day is a good time to read though. There is nothing like being able to paint a picture of a story in your head as you go along!

You say you don't have time to read? Leave a book in your car or backpack. That way you could read while standing in line, riding on the bus or waiting for a train. I like to read while at the gym while I am riding the cardio bike. Small snatches of time reading are great and even those few minutes provide benefits! There is always time to read!

Not sure what to read? Pick a movie that you liked and go to a bookstore and tell the clerk that you would like to read a book in a similar genre. Or better yet, go to the library! Do you like history? Find a book on a period of history that you find interesting. Want to learn about yourself? Pick out a self-help book. It doesn't matter what it is as long as you are reading. It's relaxing, it's comforting, and you might even learn something!

What are some of your favorite books or genres?

1)

2)

3)

4)

5)

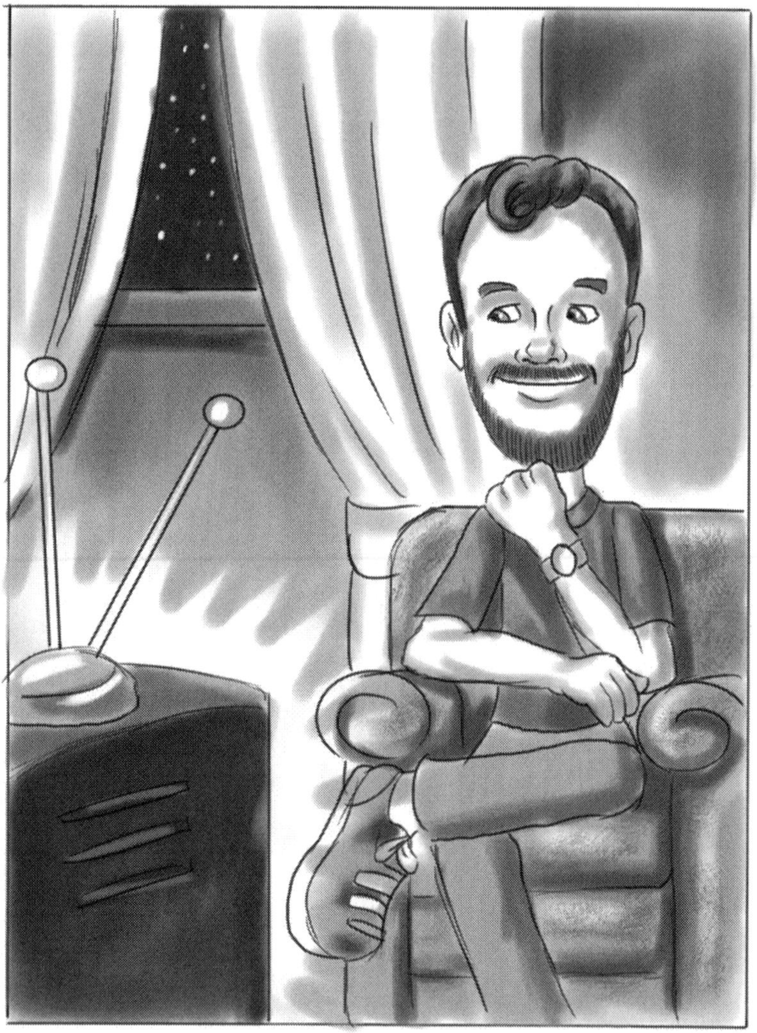

-11-

Watch an inspirational show or movie

*Only as high as I reach can I grow,
only as far as I seek can I go,
only as deep as I look can I see
only as much as I dream can I be.*
—Karen Rayn

Need a quick pick-me-up? Turn on or pick up a copy of a favorite movie or show that inspires you. This is a guaranteed fix to get you feeling upbeat, inspired and more like your true self! Watching an inspiring movie reminds us of our true selves and puts us back in touch with our true nature. We are loving, optimistic, peaceful spirits at our core. Watching an inspiring movie or the story of an inspiring person is a wonderful way to get ourselves re-aligned and back on the right track. In today's fast paced society it is easy to become sidetracked and to live in ways that don't truly suit us or our true nature. That is why it is so refreshing to see a positive, inspiring show. They make us want to reach out and be all that we can be! They get us dreaming and believing that anything is possible! They remind us of the goodness that we can find in other people.

You can personalize it also. I enjoy triathlons, so I get pumped up and inspired watching triathlon races. The Ironman races are my favorites! A lot of times I will throw them in my player while riding my bike indoors. What inspires you?

What are some of your favorite inspirational films?

_____

_____

_____

_____

_____

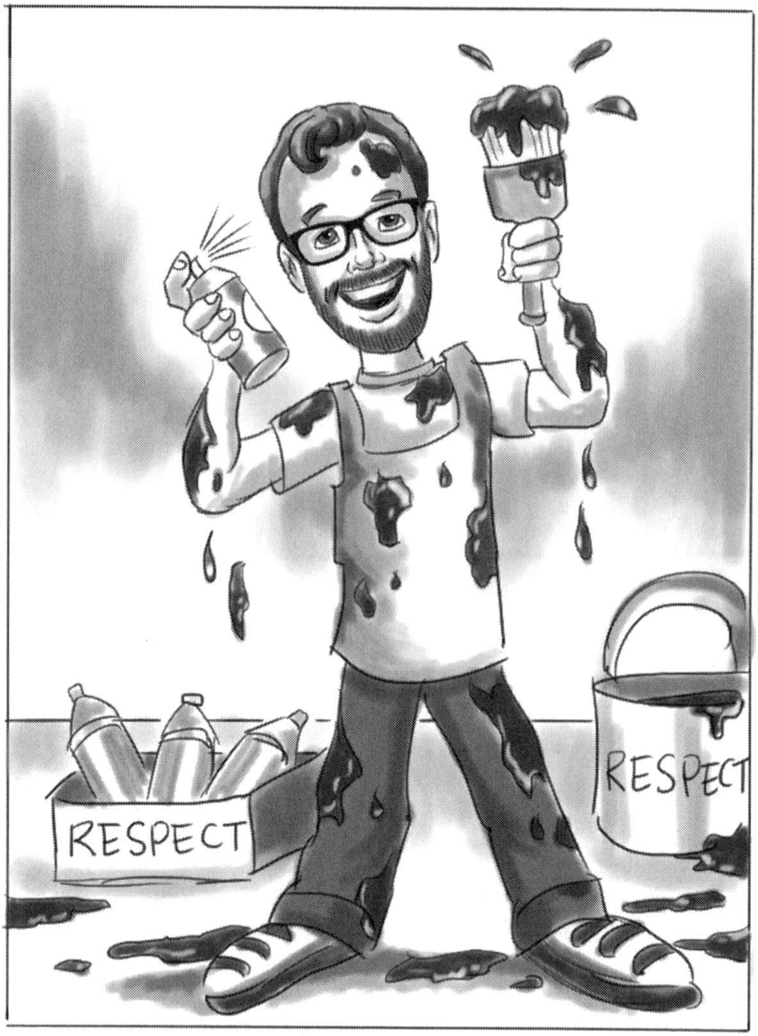
RESPECT
RESPECT

–12–

Treat yourself with respect

*Nurture your mind with great thoughts,
for you will never go any higher than you think.*
—Benjamin Disraeli

How many of you actually listen to yourself talk? I bet if you paid attention to the things you say to yourself about yourself you would be flabbergasted! Every time you say something negative about yourself, you are planting a seed of negativity. What happens is simple: you begin to live out what you tell yourself: "I can't do this, I'm no good, I am a fool for thinking that," etc. The more you tell yourself these negative affirmations, the more you will begin to believe them and live them. Treat yourself with love and respect. All of us are truly amazing beings that are capable of truly amazing things! But to tap into our creativity and our true higher selves, we have to clear out all of our negative patterns and beliefs.

Just imagine how you would feel and imagine what you could be capable of, if you just told yourself positive, loving, life affirming things. It really does make a difference. Not only will you feel better about yourself, but the type of people you will attract into your life will be much more positive. And on top of that, your confidence level will be bursting with a genuine love for yourself which can take you anywhere and allow you to do anything you want. So give yourself a pat on the back!

What are some ways you could treat yourself with respect?

1)

2)

3)

4)

5)

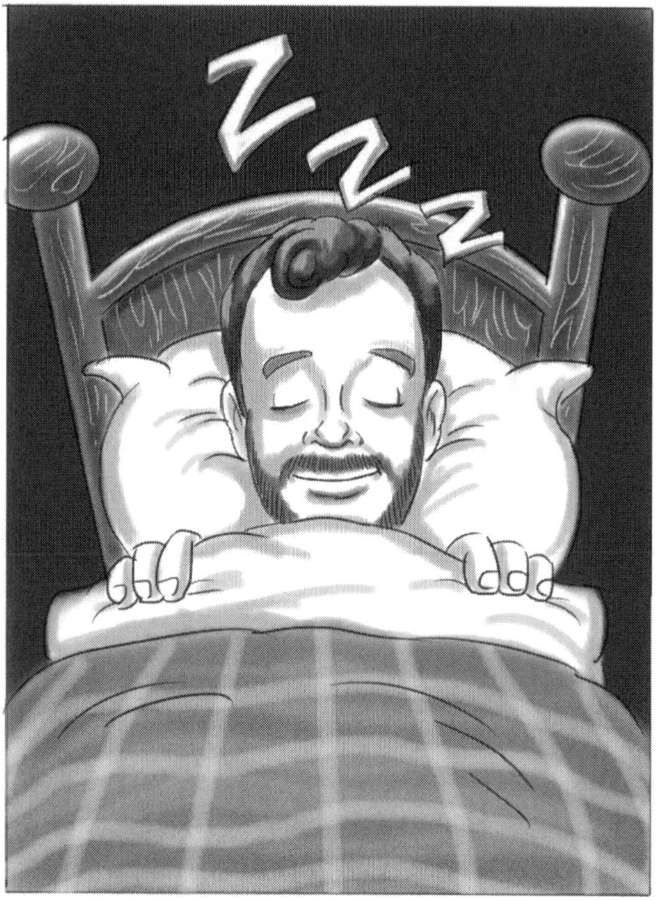
ZZZ

-13-

Get more sleep

Sleep is the golden chain that ties health and our bodies together.
—Thomas Dekker

Are you getting enough sleep? Some of you I realize don't need as much as others, but for those of you who go through the day yawning and don't think as clearly as you would like . . . get more sleep! I am at my best when I get 8 hours a night. Experiment with this. If you feel like you might need more, force yourself to get another hour or two and see if it makes a difference. And please don't think that by taking another hour or two to sleep each night out of the 24 that we have that this will make you less productive. In reality, it has been proven that those who were sleep deficient worked slower and made more mistakes along the way. So getting more sleep will in turn give you more energy, make you more productive and probably a much happier person!

I think that sleep is the number one catalyst as far as helping us stay in line with all of our other daily goals whatever they may be. For myself my goals are exercise, meditation, and eating right. When I am not getting enough sleep it makes it much harder for me to stick to my goals because I am tired and just not as centered. You might find it is the same for you!

Are you getting enough sleep?

If not, why?

What are some things you could do to allow yourself more sleep?

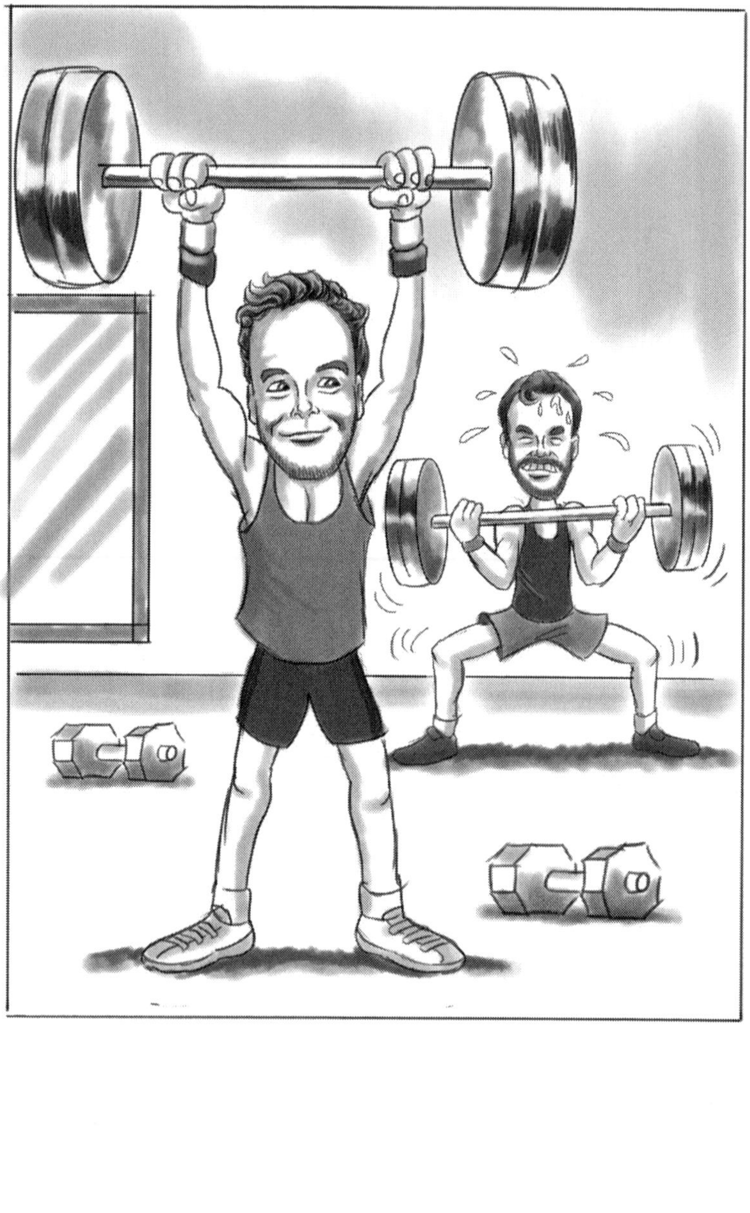

-14-

Go exercise

*We don't stop playing because we grow old,
we grow old because we stop playing.*
—GEORGE BERNARD SHAW

Need a little more energy throughout the day? Want to lose a few unwanted pounds? Want to think more clearly and be more productive? Want to feel better about yourself? The answer is simple, get some exercise!

There are many ways to make exercise a part of your lifestyle and it is very important to start out at a level that works for you. If you are just beginning, it could be as easy as going for a walk 3 days a week. The key is to make whatever you do a habit!

Not sure where to start? Your local fitness club is probably a great starting place. They would certainly have knowledgeable staff available to help you get a program going based on your goals. Don't want to join a gym? No problem, just go on the Internet and search out what you might be interested in and then learn about it. It is very important though that if you are new at a particular sport or exercise that you know what you are doing. Especially if you begin to use weights or start up a weight lifting program. Proper form is essential to avoid injuries. There are plenty of other ways to get exercise that don't require special knowledge or a set of skills that you might not have. Gardening, swimming (or just splashing around!), going to a park and throwing a Frisbee, and, like I mentioned earlier, walking.

So what are you waiting for? There are no excuses! Your body, your mind and your confidence will be glad you did!

What are some possible ways you could get some exercise?

1)

2)

3)

4)

5)

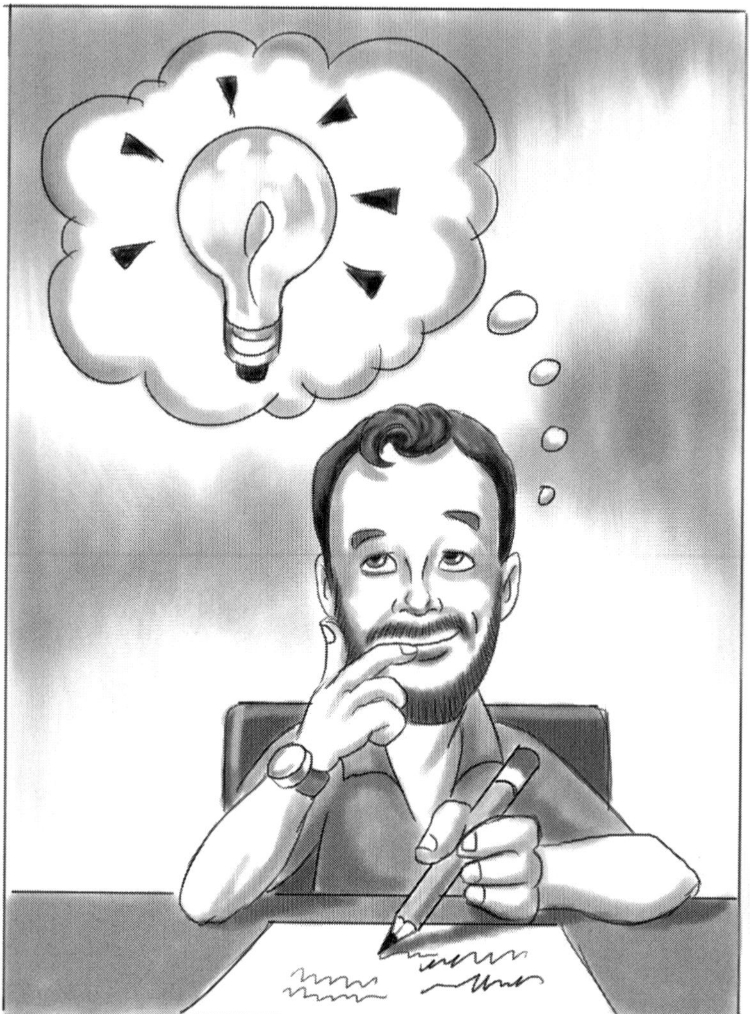

–15–

Write down your thoughts

*Worry is like a rocking chair—
it gives you something to do but won't get you anywhere.*
—Unknown Author

How many times have you had something rolling around in your head that was bothering you? It is a very common occurrence and it can affect your moods, your productivity at work, and even your sleep. Maybe this thing rolling around in your head was a misunderstanding you had with another person. Maybe you have a presentation coming up at your job, or a test on the horizon at school. It doesn't really matter what, just that it was keeping you from being present and centered.

My advice to you is to write down what is bothering you on a piece of paper or in a journal. Let it go! By writing down what is bothering you, you are essentially identifying your problem. And by identifying your problem, you are able to release it from your mind and hopefully that will stop the nagging, sometimes debilitating, effects of what is bothering you. I realize it doesn't solve what you are dealing with, but by confronting it and identifying it, you are putting it front and center and accepting it. This can be a big relief to your mental makeup! And by writing it down, you no longer have to let it wriggle around in your head, and it allows you to move on and relax. Let the piece of paper deal with the worry!

Do you journal?

Are you a note writer?

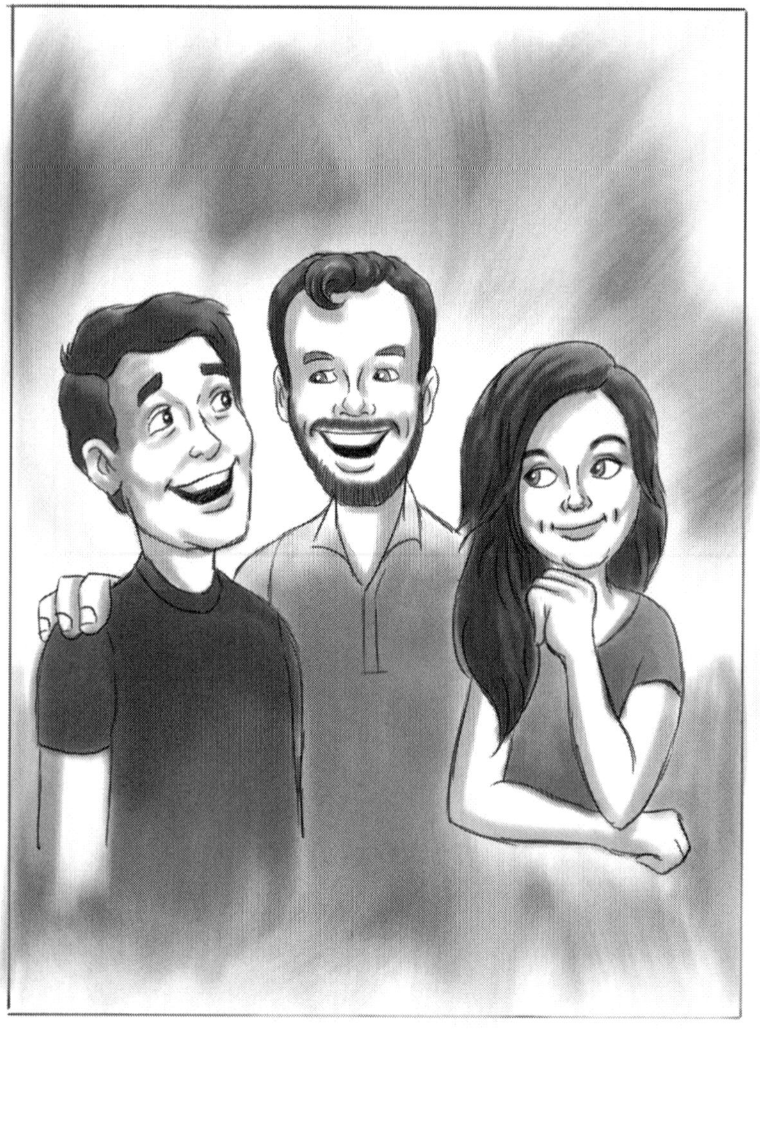

-16-

Hang out with positive people

Where there are friends, there is wealth.
—Titus Muccius Plautus

It's as simple as it sounds. If you strive to be happy, inspired and motivated like most of us do, don't you think you would want to associate with people that aspire to the same goals? Just being around someone who loves life and has a positive outlook on things has a way of generating energy in others. I know being around optimistic people motivates me to be even more positive!

Try to think of some times when you were around someone who was negative, complained a lot and was quite unhappy. It's a big energy drain, isn't it? They leave you feeling tired and spent. It's tough to be around a bunch of complainers. Our true natural state is one of love and positivity. That's why we feel so connected and in the flow when we are with those people that exude positive characteristics!

So go strike up a conversation with an enthusiastic stranger or someone you enjoy talking with. There is no better way to learn, connect and be in the flow of life. Not to mention it broadens our horizons. It will always leave you feeling refreshed and positive! You would also be surprised at the synchronistic events that occur while chatting with like-minded people. The connections, the similarities, the shared experiences all come out while sharing with someone else.

Where are some places that you could meet or surround yourself with positive people?

A few suggestions:
-Local Meet Up groups
-Book Clubs
-Hobby Clubs
-Fitness Center/exercise class

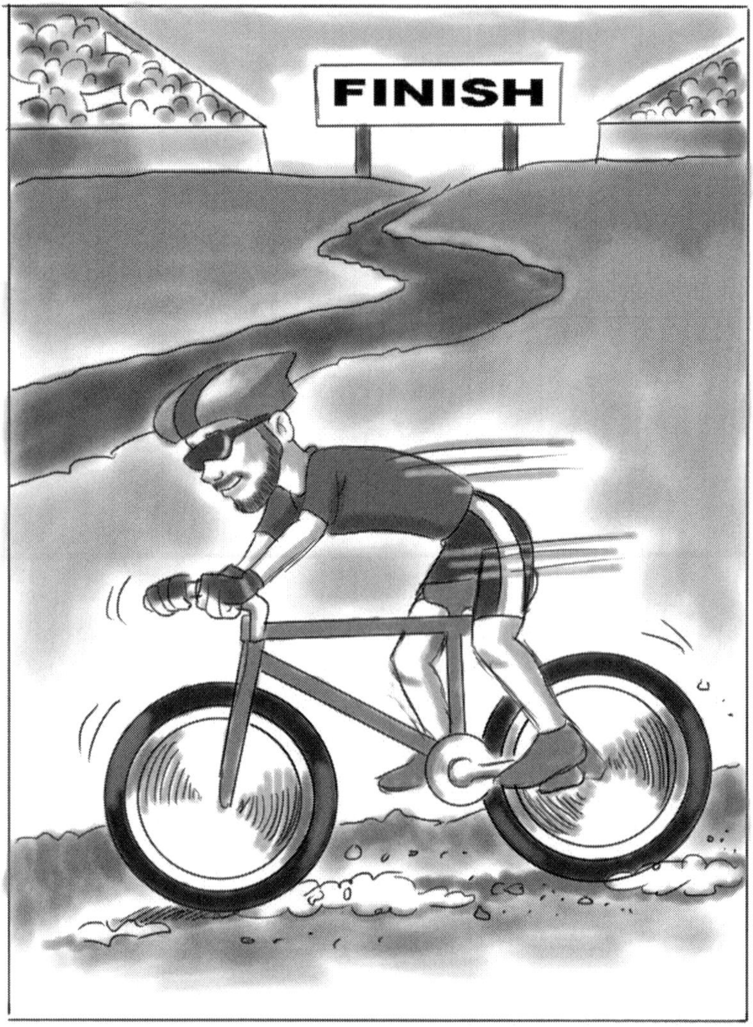
FINISH

–17–

Set a goal and follow through with it

In the confrontation between the stream and the rock, the stream always wins, not through strength but by perseverance.
—H. Jackson Brown

Who wants to make some positive changes in their lives? I think we all do! Or at least I hope we all do. For most of us, getting started is the hardest part of initiating any new change into our lives, whether it be starting a diet or exercise plan, or looking for a new job. But if we can get the ball rolling and work to make our new plan a habit, then it becomes much easier.

I think a lot of people have red flags pop up into their heads whenever they think about initiating change. The negative self-talk begins and past failures creep up into their mindset. We need to eliminate that negative self-talk and replace the failure mindset with one that is success-oriented.

How do we accomplish this? Set some small goals, something very attainable. Then make sure you follow through with them! Small goals allow us to grow into a new habit which then allows it to become a permanent part of our lives. For example, let's say you want to eat healthier. Instead of just radically changing your diet all at once, begin to make subtle changes to it, so you don't set yourself up for failure or a real struggle. Feel good about the subtle changes you make, get used to them and then make more changes, one at a time. By easing into your goal, you are able to become successful. Success breeds success! Keep building on it. You can do it!

What are some of your current goals?

1)

2)

3)

What are some of your past successes with goal setting?

1)

2)

3)

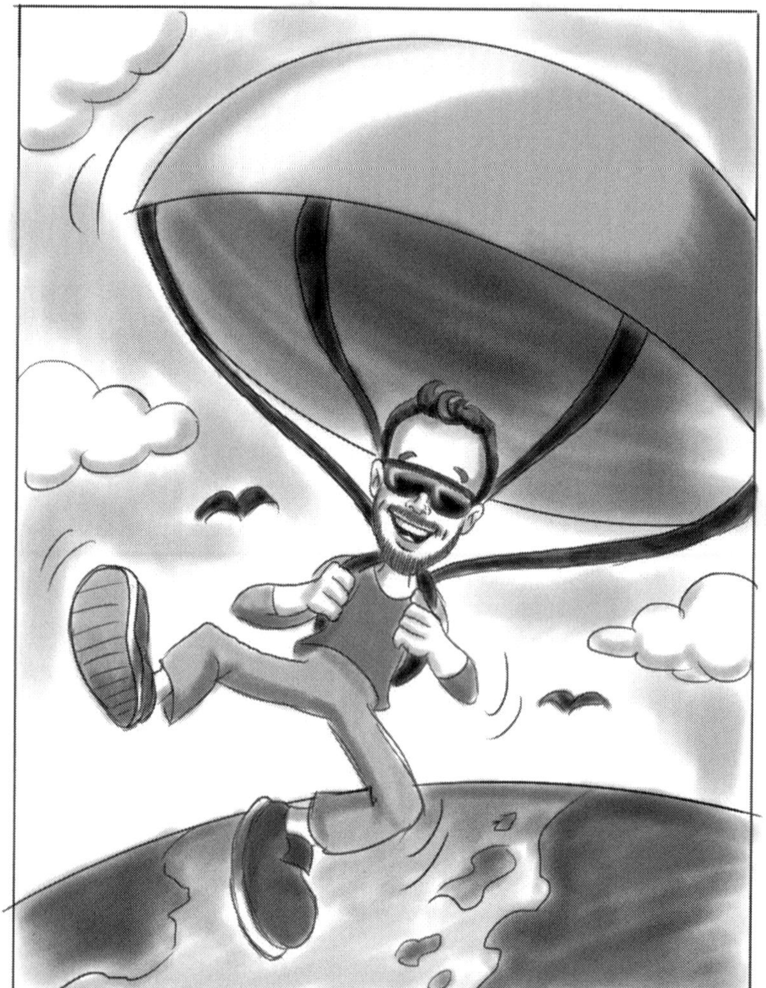

-18-

Try something new, take a chance

*Our deepest fears are like dragons,
guarding our deepest treasure.*
—Rainer Maria Rilke

Are you in a bit of a rut? Feeling like you are going through the motions day after day? Snap out of it and try something new! We aren't meant to be stagnant. We were put here to learn, have fun and grow! The world should be your oyster!

What is it that you would like to do that you haven't tried yet? A certain sport? A new hairstyle? A specific class at the local community college? How about learning a new language and then planning a trip so you can put to practice what you have just learned. The possibilities are endless!

The key is to just do something different. Expand your horizons. Wake up your spirit! Take a chance and set aside your fears. What do you have to lose? Remember, our true nature is geared for this!

What are some things you have wanted to go do or try?

1)

2)

3)

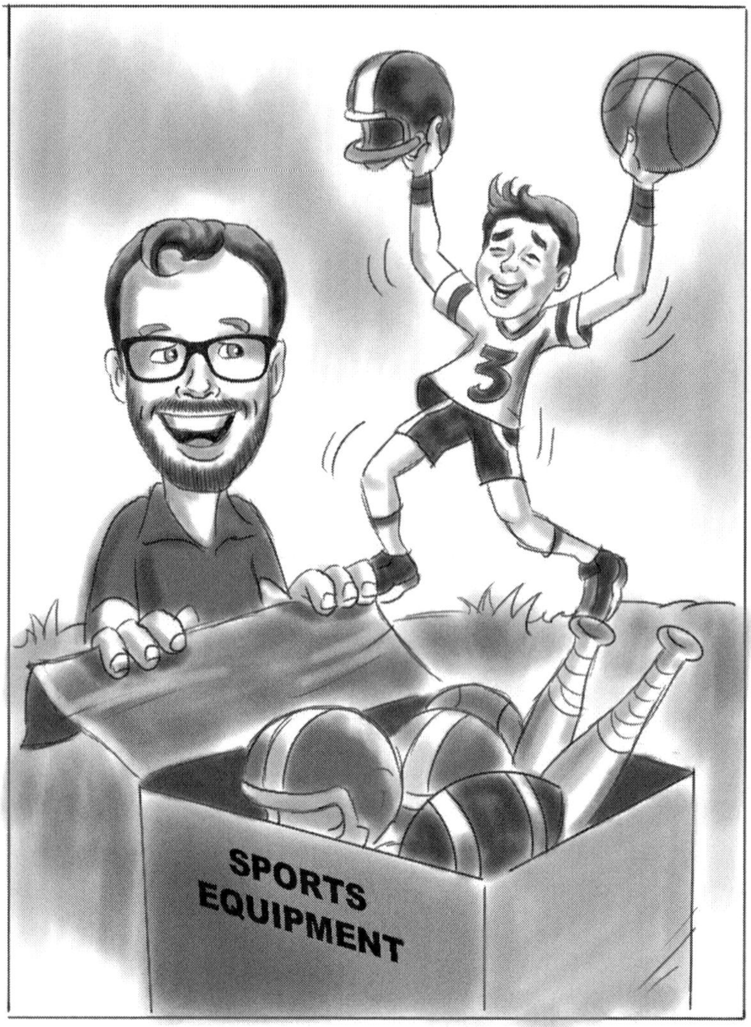
3
SPORTS
EQUIPMENT

-19-

Give

If you want happiness for an hour, take a nap.
If you want happiness for a day, go fishing.
If you want happiness for a year, inherit a fortune.
If you want happiness for a lifetime, help somebody.
—CHINESE PROVERB

How does it make you feel when you help someone out? It feels good, right? It doesn't matter if you are helping a friend move or spending the afternoon down at the local food bank. It feels good! I have always said that the full measure of our personal happiness is dictated by how much we offer of ourselves in helping others. It's simple: give. Giving can occur in many different ways. One way is volunteering your time somewhere. Be a coach for a youth sports league. Go read to young children in a school-sponsored program. Be a friend to some seniors at an assisted living facility. Mentor a teenager through the many different wonderful programs that are out there. Help someone who is struggling to get back on their feet.

Another way to give is financially. If you have the means, there are hundreds and hundreds of worthy programs that depend on private funds to run their operations. Food kitchens for the homeless, wheelchair programs for the disabled, sports programs for youth, are just the tip of the iceberg.

And finally, another way to give is simply through donating your quality used goods. If you have something that might be of value to someone else and you aren't using it, why not donate it? Clothes are one of the first things that come to mind.

Whichever way you choose to give, it doesn't matter. Just do it! Giving offers us perspective on how blessed we truly are. You will feel better, you will be helping others, you will be doing the right thing, and you will be making a positive impact in your community and the world!

What are some ways that you could give and be of service?

1)

2)

3)

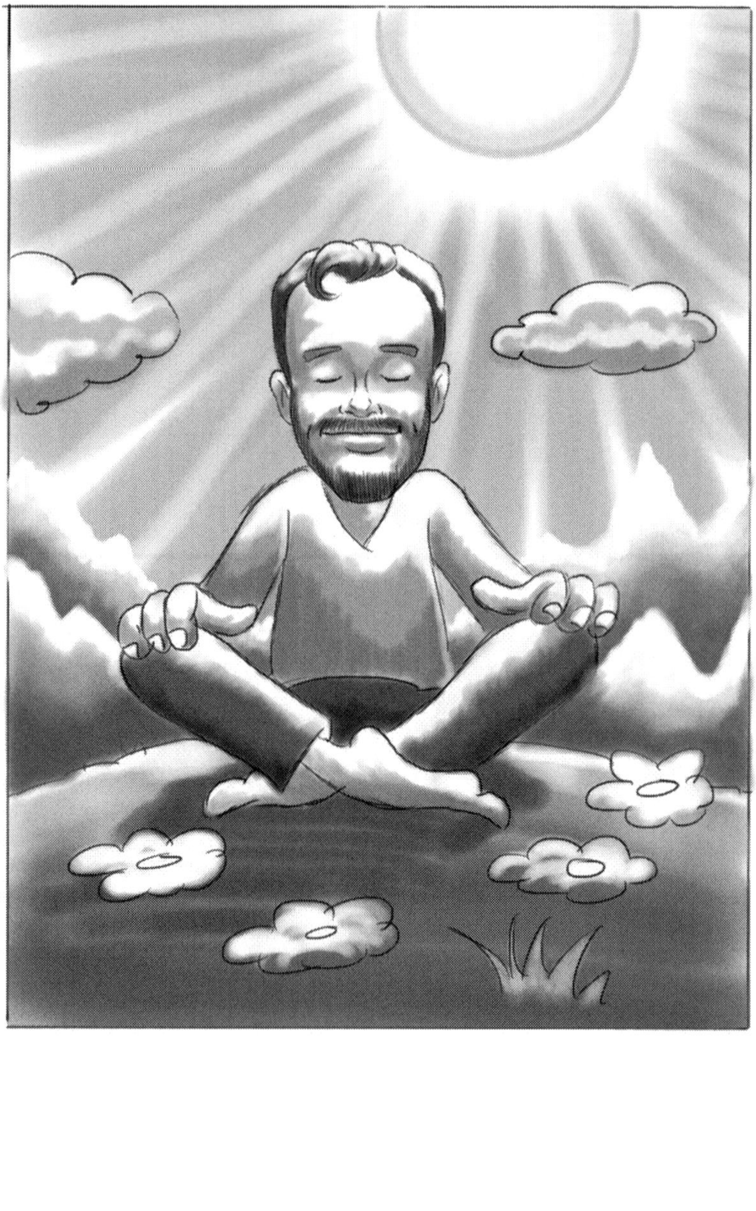

–20–

Meditate

Seek truth in meditation, not in moldy books.
Look in the sky to find the moon, not in the pond.
—PERSIAN PROVERB

Do you want to feel calmer, carry less stress, have more energy and be less anxious? You might want to try meditation. Meditation, you say? I know this may be a bit of a stretch for some of you, but meditation has been life changing for many people including myself. I am now more relaxed, less anxious, and much easier-going than I used to be, since I started this practice about 2 years ago. According to Dr. Wayne Dyer, "Meditation is simply the art of being quiet with yourself and shutting down the constant monologue that fills the inner space of your being. And that inner monologue or noise is a shield preventing you from knowing the highest self." In other words, while meditating we are able to give our brain a rest from the busy life and schedule that most of us lead. Which in turn helps us to feel more rested, balanced and centered. Who wouldn't want to feel that way?

There are many forms of meditation and many different ways to meditate. Some people prefer chanting, while others sit silently focusing on their breathing. I recommend doing an Internet search to learn more about the varieties of meditation and what might be best for you. You might want to experiment with a few different styles and stick with the one that resonates for you. There are many wonderful books out on meditation as well. One that I would recommend is *Manifest Your Destiny* by Dr. Wayne Dyer.

Consistency is very important when starting any meditation program. I realize that it might seem a bit out of your comfort level while you are getting started, but please stick with it. It will soon become easier and feel very natural. I enjoy meditating twice a day: once in the morning for about 15 minutes and once before bedtime for the same amount of time. It is something I look forward to each day.

I encourage you to think about giving meditation a try. You have nothing to lose except your stress and anxiety levels!

Some other ways to fall into a meditative state:
1) Walking/hiking
2) Exercise
3) Listening to certain types of music
4) Drawing/painting
5) Riding a bike
6) Working with your hands/pottery/model cars or airplanes
7) Arts and crafts
8) Gardening
9) Playing a musical instrument
10) Sitting in nature

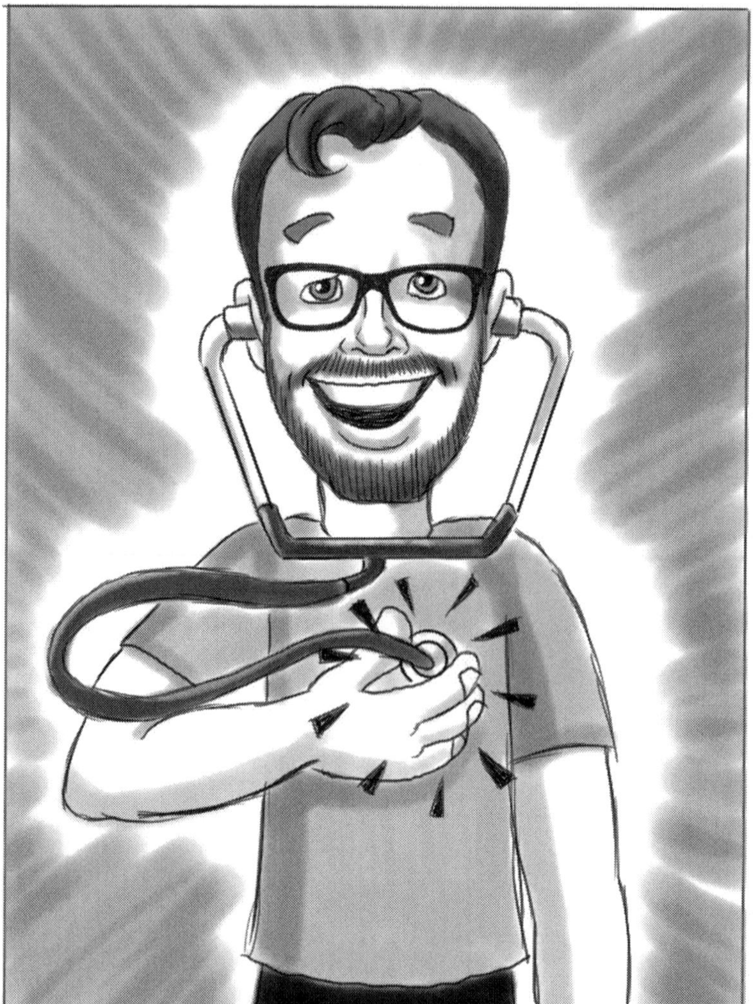

-21-

Listen to your heart

One sees clearly only with the heart.
Anything essential is invisible to the eyes.
—Antoine de Saint-Exupery

Have you ever been to a store and just stood there looking at an item that you just could not make up your mind on? I think we have all been in that position at one time or another. You know, just standing there and running through all the pro's and con's of trying to decide whether or not you should make the purchase. If it is taking you that long to decide, it probably isn't the right purchase for you. It could be because of the price of the item, the fact that you already had one, or that you really didn't need one. No matter the reason, your uncertainty indicates your heart and mind are in an epic battle! Let your mind rest, and let your heart takeover. The reason being . . . it is always right! If this purchase is meant to be, your heart will be singing and you will feel really good about the item and making the purchase. But when indecision plagues you, your mind is fighting to come up with some very good reasons for you to walk out of that store with it. But deep down, you know it isn't right because of the feeling you receive in your gut or heart. It isn't on board with your mind.

    Listening to your heart works in all facets of your life: A positive or negative feeling you get about a person you just met, whether or not you want to take a particular job you are offered, or feelings you are having dealing with your boyfriend or girlfriend. Honoring your feelings isn't always the easiest route to take or the most popular. But I can tell you it is the right route. Being honest with yourself is the most important thing you can do. I want you to walk out of that store whistling a happy tune, not dealing with buyer's remorse!

Are you listening to your intuitive hunches?

Do your trust your intuitive feelings?

If not, why?

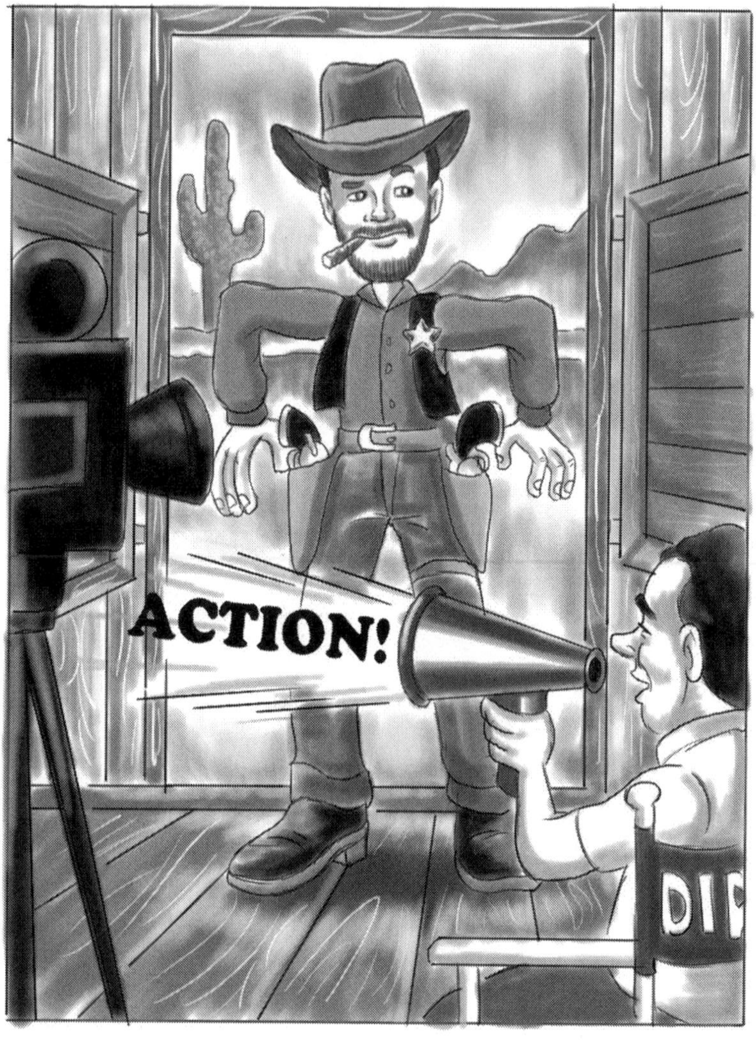
ACTION!

–22–

Do what you love

*There's no scarcity of opportunity
to make a living at what you love.
There is only a scarcity of resolve to make it happen.*
—Dr. Wayne Dyer

Do what you love. It is as simple as it sounds. How many of you do things just because we think we should? Or because these things have become habit? I think most of us are guilty of this at one point or another. How we find ourselves in these situations can vary and there are as many reasons as there are particular examples. Let's use work for starters. Maybe you took a job out of perceived necessity and then became complacent at it. Or maybe you stayed at this job out of fear. Maybe you hopped right into a particular job market out of college because you thought you were expected to. Or maybe you felt familial pressure to carry on the family business even though it didn't inspire you. All of these situations could find a person not doing what they love. Unfortunately you probably found yourself in a state of just going through the motions and not enjoying life like it was meant to be enjoyed.

Let's use a different example. Do you find yourself always agreeing to do what your friends or significant other wants to do? Why is that? Does it bother you? Give and take is an important part of any relationship. Whether it be in a friendship or a marriage. But it is also very important that you be able to do the things that you love and enjoy so that you can truly feel the full capacity of who you are and what you are about. If you aren't doing what you love, then you need to start making it happen. As you do, your world will come alive. You will feel happier, lighter, more fulfilled and there will be a true excitement about your purpose.

So if bike riding makes you feel alive, then do it! If you truly love to knit while listening to The Beatles, then do it! If you feel like you might like to change careers and work with troubled youth, do it! You have nothing to lose except for your present confusion and unhappiness. Think of all you have to gain: happiness, a sense of purpose, and an optimistic future. Do what you love! If it makes you happy then we all benefit!

What are some things that you truly love to do?

1)

2)

3)

4)

5)

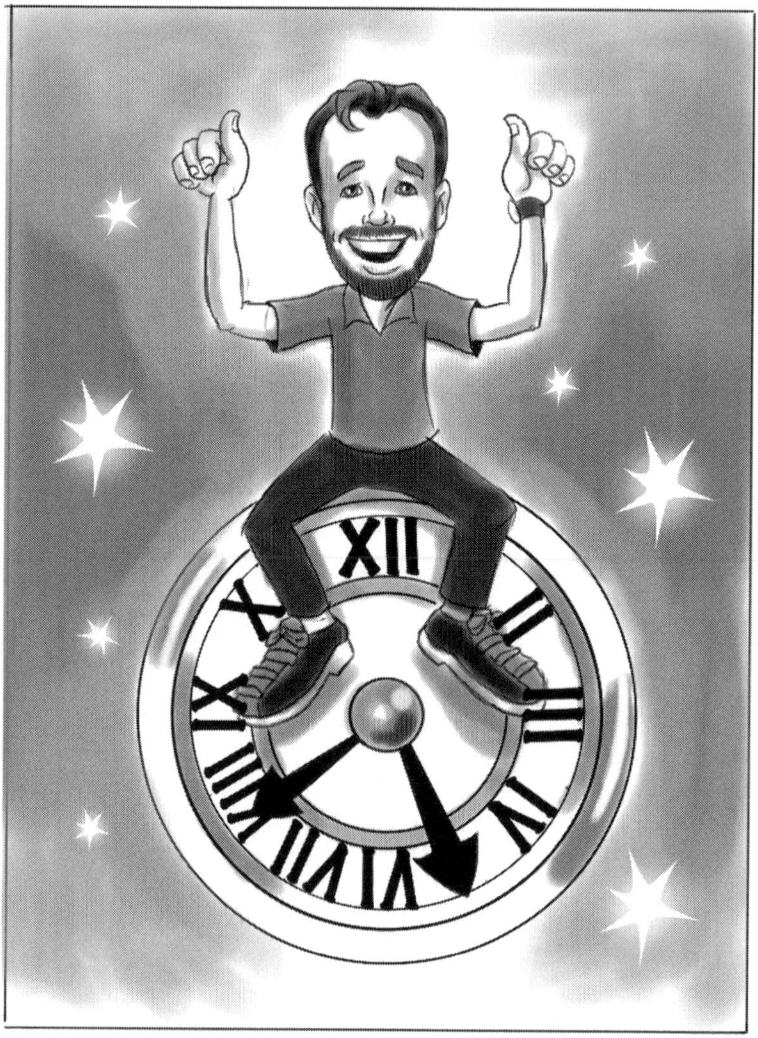

–23–

Live in the moment— be present

If you surrender completely to the moments as they pass, you live more richly those moments.
—Anne Morrow Lindbergh

Have you ever been doing something (anything) and not totally been present because you were worrying about something that had happened in the past or might happen in the future? We all certainly have. When we do this, we don't allow ourselves to fully take in or enjoy the actual moment when it is happening. Guilt or fear creep in and cause us much heaviness when more often than not, there is absolutely no basis for our guilty or fearful feelings. What is key to remember when finding ourselves in this situation is that neither the past nor the future are real. Only the now is truly available to us.

To quote John Demartini from his wonderful book *The Breakthrough Experience,* "Time consists of both future and past, neither of which can ever be in the now. The past holds memory, is emotionally based, and is dominated by the emotion labeled guilt. The future holds imagination, is also emotionally based, and is dominated by the emotion labeled fear. The loving essence of your true spirit is spaceless and timeless presence."

In other words, be in the caring, loving flow that life is meant to be—in the now. Where we create the life of our choosing. Where we manifest our hopes and dreams into reality. Our true nature is based in the now. So why would we ever want to do anything but live in the moment or be present?

By living in the moment we free ourselves from worry, guilt, fear, anger, resentment and uncertainty. By being present we can focus on the task at hand and not about something that already has happened, or that has yet to be. The past is the past and the future has yet to be played out. And since thoughts are things, we want to focus our attention on the present and be positive, not the past where we may have experienced hurt or confusion or the future and our potential uncertainty or fear.

I realize that this takes some work, because it is very easy to slip into the past and play out scenarios in our mind that we may have wished hadn't happened, or had gone a different way. That is only natural, but it weakens our ability to create the now that we truly want. Try to embrace what happened in the past and be thankful for the learning experience it provided. You must come to accept it, so you can move on. So focus on the here and now. Be present! Live in the moment!

Do you find yourself worrying about the past? The future?

If so, why?

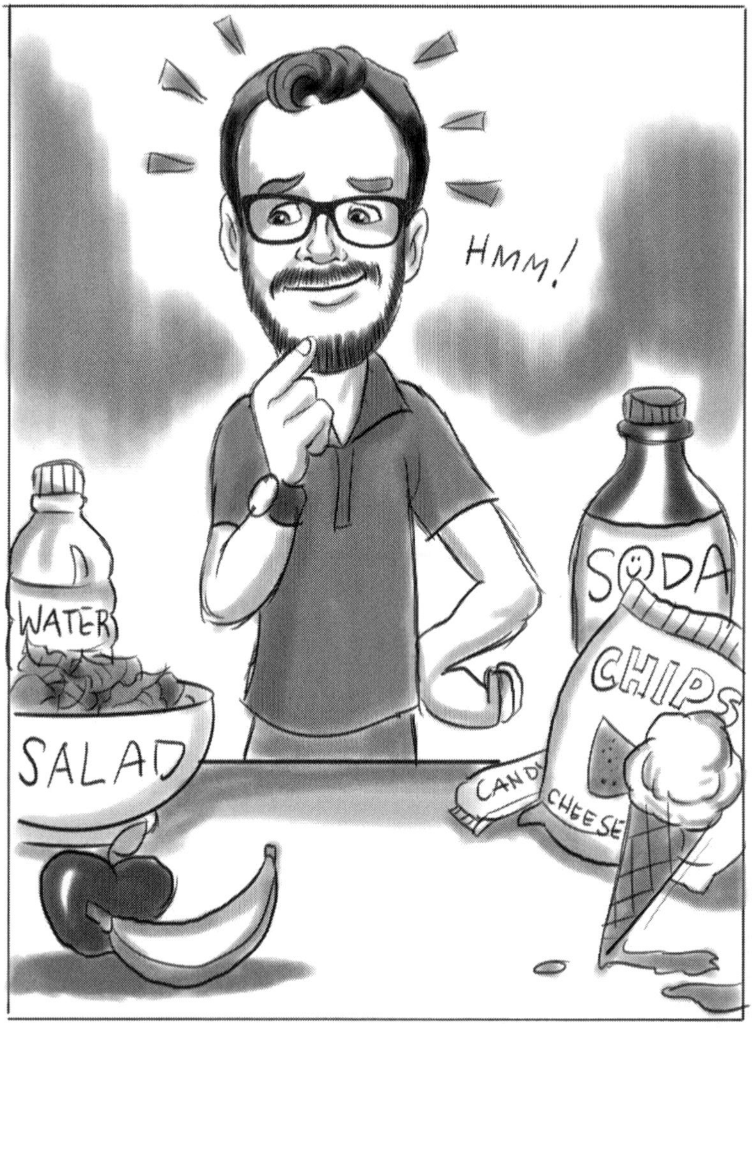
HMM!
WATER
SODA
CHIPS
SALAD
CANDY
CHEESE

-24-

Eat better, eat less

*You must begin to think of yourself
as the person you want to be.*
—David Viscott

How many of us pay attention to how we feel after having a meal or a snack? My guess is not many. Really listen to your body after you eat. It definitely is talking to you. How does it talk to you? Primarily through your energy level. If you are constantly struggling for energy during the day and you are feeling very sluggish after you eat, then you are probably not putting the best food that you could into your body. If you listen to your body it can tell you what works for it and what doesn't.

What is good food? Obviously a nice balance of fruits, vegetables, grains, milk/dairy and meat/beans/fish/nuts.

Generally, if you strive for moderation in some foods, like red meat or others that tend to be high in fat, then you should be fine. And as you begin to eat better, you will notice that you like the way you feel after you eat.

Stick to live food. Stay away from food that is processed. You will be able to continue on with your day feeling light on your feet and energized, not sluggish and needing to sit down for a bit. The foods to definitely stay away from are the fast food entrees that have become a staple of our nation's diet as well as any other processed high in fat/calorie offering that you might find in your grocery store. There is very little nutrition offered and I can guarantee you very little sustainable energy for the consumer. Pay attention to how you feel after you eat a fast food meal. There might be a few offerings that have some nutritional value on their menu but for the most part, no.

Another key to feeling better and more energized is to eat less. We have been trained to super-size everything and that is not ok. Most of us eat more than we need to during our meals. Try to cut back a bit on your portion sizes. Psychologically it might be hard, but nutritionally I can tell you that you will be just fine. Like any other habit, it will take a little bit of time, work and concentration to make the change. But if you make the change, I promise you that you will feel better, have more energy and maybe even lose a few pounds.

If you want to make some changes, just go online and type in healthy eating and you will find many sites dedicated to helping people learn about their eating habits. You have absolutely nothing to lose! What have you got to gain? More energy, a body that runs more efficiently, a longer life, higher self esteem and clothes that fit better, just to name a few. You can do it!

What are some healthy foods that you enjoy?

1)

2)

3)

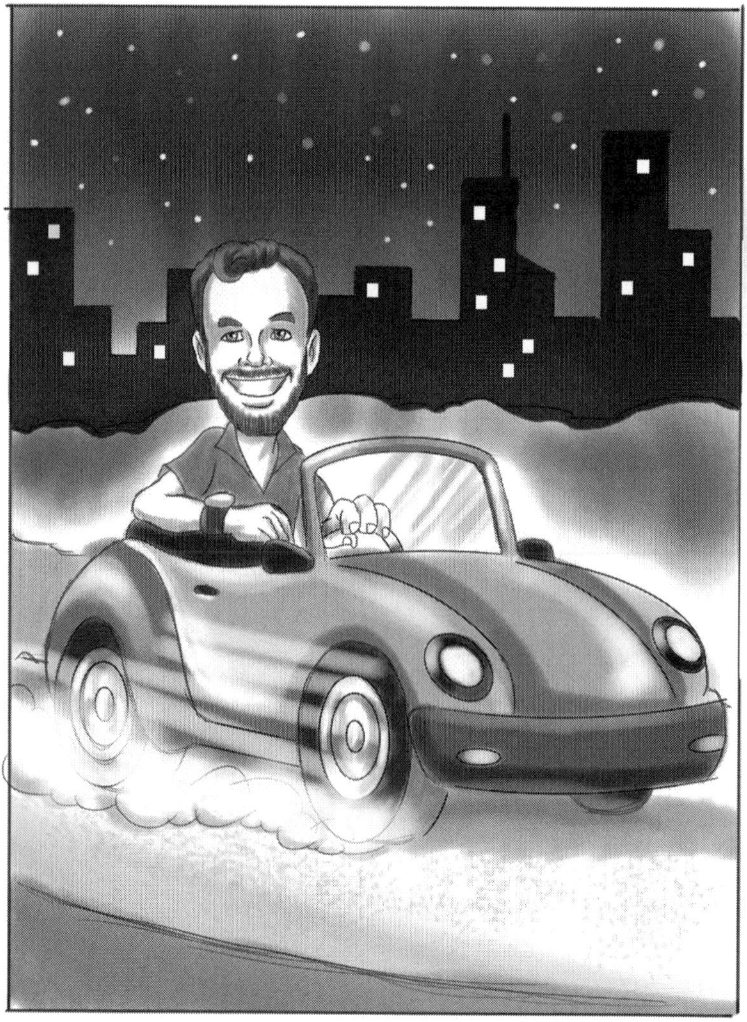

−25−

Leave 10 minutes early

A first rate organizer is never in a hurry. He is never late. He always keeps up his sleeve a margin for the unexpected.
—Arnold Bennett

How often do you find yourself rushing late to work or someplace else that you need to be? How does it make you feel? Stressed? Angry? Guilty? You know there is a very simple thing that you can do to eliminate all of those unwanted feelings that come from being rushed. Why not try leaving 10 minutes early?

I realize that there is the occasional time when we are running late due to reasons out of our control, but for the majority of the time, it doesn't have to be that way. Why not just try heading out the door a few minutes earlier than usual? You would be amazed at how peaceful and restful your drive into work can be! If you miss a traffic light, it becomes no big deal. If you get stuck at a railroad crossing, same thing, no big deal! Knowing that you have a few extra minutes will help relax you and make your commute so much smoother, easier and less stressful.

When I started leaving 10 minutes early to go to work, I noticed the difference immediately. I arrived at work feeling so much more peaceful and balanced. I was ready to start the day! Prior to leaving 10 minutes early, I would be scrambling in to work, carrying a lot of worry and stress. More often than not, I would start the day off feeling a bit behind the eight ball. Not a good way to go.

So if you can allow yourself those 10 extra minutes each time you need to go someplace, I would recommend that you do so. You will be a safer driver, you will feel at ease during your commute, and you will arrive at your destination in a much better mood. Probably feeling very balanced and centered!

How often are you on time?

Is being late an issue for you?

If so, why?

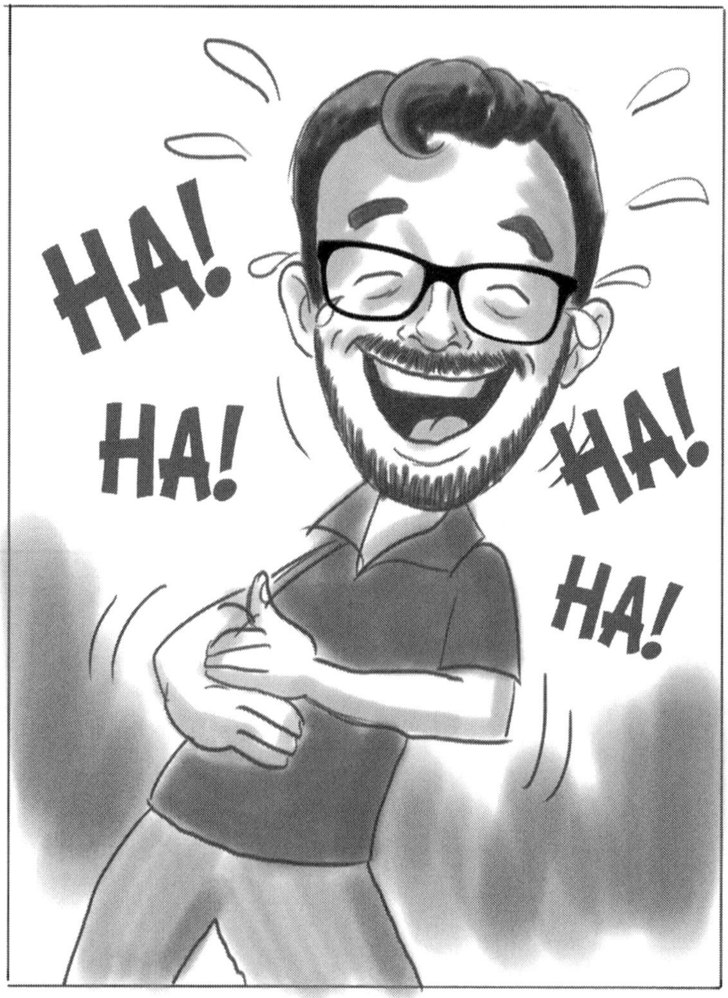
HA!
HA!
HA!
HA!

–26–

Laugh

Laughter is instant sunshine.
—G. Brian Benson

Have you ever had one of those days where nothing seemed to be going right and then all of a sudden you saw or heard something really funny that just totally turned your attitude around because you started to laugh? I am sure we all have! Laughter really is the best medicine!

"The most wasted of all days is one without laughter," says E.E. Cummings. How could we not agree with that? To laugh is to feel alive. To laugh with another is to be spiritually connected with them. Laughter brings hope. Laughter brings relief. Laughter heals our bodies. Laughter brings people together. Why would anyone not want to laugh? I think the best way to have a laugh is to share it with another person. There becomes an instant bond between the two people that really is quite heartfelt.

Luckily for us, there are plenty of wonderful places to search out a laugh if we need one: movies, TV, the Internet, books, magazines, politics, friends, life experiences, and the list goes on and on.

So what are you waiting for? Go rent your favorite comedy movie or read the comic section in the newspaper. Or better yet, go grab a friend and share a laugh with them! Your quality of life will instantly improve!

What makes you laugh?

Are you allowing yourself enough laughter and humor in your life?

How could you include more?

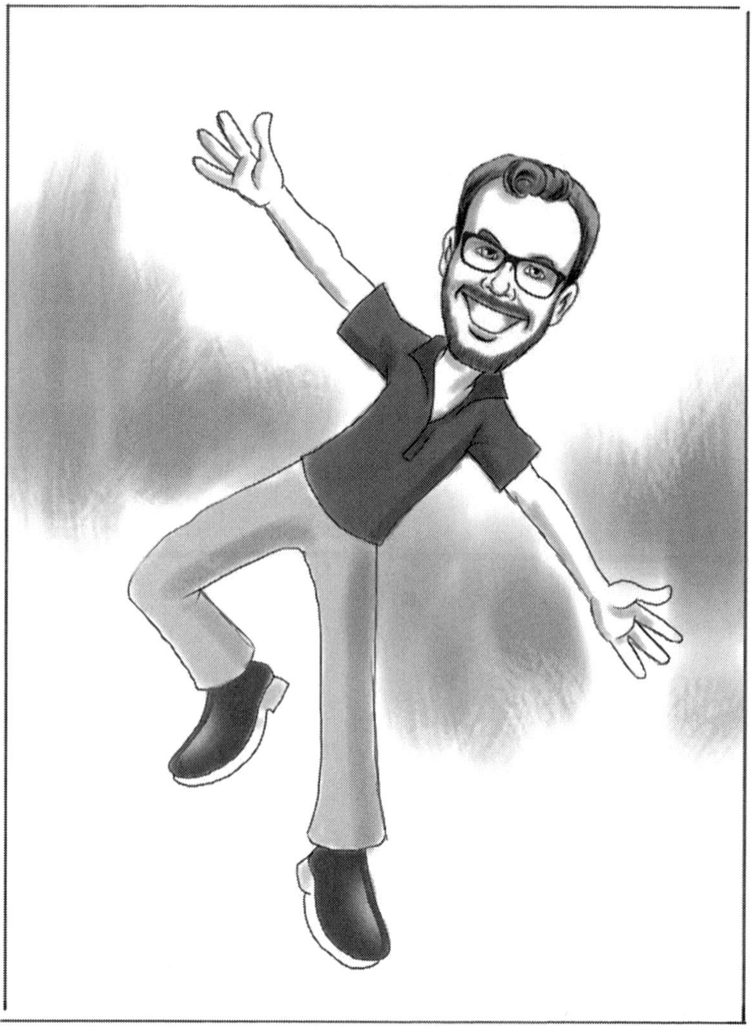

–26 ½–

Other ideas to help you stay balanced

Pure and simple, balance is happiness.
—Dr. Frederick Lenz

Here are a handful of other things that you can do to add some balance, fun and centeredness to your life. They are all self-explanatory and not in any particular order. If you are anything like me, sometimes you might initially raise your eyebrows at a new idea or way of doing something. I can understand that. Some of my ideas may make you do that. But if you have an inkling of interest or an open mind, I invite you to try some or all of these. I think they are solid and will help you create the balance that you want to make permanent in your life.

- watch less television
- take a trip (get away)

- take a relaxing bath
- try yoga (it's great for building strength and creating flexibility)
- get a massage
- do your best to be your best
- light some candles
- continue to learn and grow
- garden
- get creative
- let go of judgment
- learn patience
- bring some flowers and plants into your home
- ride your bike to work
- support your local vendors/stores
- be a good/positive example for someone
- just be yourself

What are some of your favorite ways to stay in balance?

1)

2)

3)

4)

5)

Final thought

We are cups, constantly and quietly being filled.
The trick is, knowing how to tip ourselves over
and let the beautiful stuff out.
—Ray Bradbury

There are many different paths and each one of ours is different. Do not feel that you need to follow another's. Create your own. That is the way that it is supposed to be and that is the only way that you will find true happiness. Listen to your heart and believe in your journey. Make it special! Do what you love, be thankful for all of your gifts and continue to grow.

All of your learning experiences up to this point (tough and easy) have made you who you are and have set the stage for the rest of your wonderful life. Be proud of who you are and strive to be the best you can be.

Greatness is already in us! We just need to peel away a few layers and reconnect! By implementing some or all of my cues that I have listed in this book, you are well on your way to being the best you that you can be! I believe in you. It's time to start believing in yourself!

Believing Eyes

Limber thoughts of trust present
New ways to live heaven sent

Our hearts and minds a mix to stir
Which yields results inner and pure

Each path is new yet spoken for
To unlock our duty we must open the door

To listen and hear through believing eyes
And not be afraid when old ways die

To tap your highest, there's no greater score
Inspiration, motivation and love evermore

G. Brian Benson
3-20-07

Acknowledgments

There are many people that I would like to thank for helping me put this together. First of all, I would like to thank all of my awesome, kind, loving friends who get what life is about and who have always been there for me with a kind word, some encouragement or a laugh. And a special thank you to those of you who read some of the earlier drafts of *Brian's List* and gave me your honest feedback and support. I appreciate each and every one of you!

I would like to thank Sandra Haven at Bristol Services Intl. in Carlsborg, Washington for her editing services, wonderful ideas and great sense of humor!

I would like to thank my very inspiring and dear friend from up North, Sandy Struss. Sandy is a wonderful writer, motivational speaker and a true beacon of light put here on earth to bring ease and cheer to all she comes across. I can't thank her enough for her kind words and support.

I would like to thank my fantastic illustrator Paul Hernandez whose work has always rocked and graced many of my other projects.

I would like to thank Lisa Hepner of Portland, Oregon whose work through the years has inspired me. Lisa gave me some great ideas about self-publishing and lots of encouragement.

I would also like to thank Jennifer Omner of ALL Publications. Jennifer did the layout for this book as well as helped me design the original cover. She is a true professional and was helpful in every way. You can reach Jennifer at www.allpublications.com.

Last but certainly not least, I would like to thank my family. My parents and brother and sister have always been very supportive of me through the years. They were always there for me and cheered me on whether I was doing a triathlon, riding my bike across the country or taking a leap into the unknown to move and create a new space for myself in a new city. Thanks and much love to all of you. I am your biggest cheerleader, as I know you are mine. And a special thanks to my son Michael. Although we are a bit different in our likes and ways, I want you to know that you make me very proud and I have all the confidence in the world in you!

Other Works

Also by Brian:

Habits for Success – Inspired Ideas to Help You Soar

Lucy and Chester's Amazing Adventures!

Steve the Alien

Finding Your Voice

To learn more about Brian, his coaching, podcast, TEDx presentation, or to sign up for his newsletter please go to: www.gbrianbenson.com

You can follow Brian @

Twitter - @gbrianbenson
Instagram - @gbrianbenson
Facebook - @gbrianbensonmedia
YouTube - @gbrianbenson

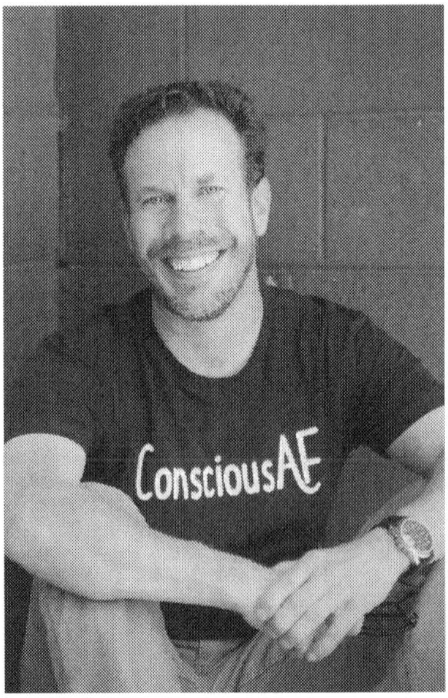
ConsciousAF

About Brian

G. Brian Benson's mission is to wake up the world with conscious, thought-provoking media that inspires. As founder of Reawaken Media, Brian an award-winning and #1 best-selling self-improvement and children's author, coach, actor, filmmaker and TEDx speaker, knows the value of trusting intuition and wants to share his own personal journey of self-growth, discovery and accomplishment to help others re-connect with their own personal truths to live an authentic and fulfilling life. As a 4x Ironman triathlete, Brian knows the value of hard work and never giving up on his dreams, a message he shares with audiences through each of his creative expressions. Brian has a brand new book coming out winter of 2018 called "Habits for Success – Inspired Ideas to Help You Soar" through Mango Publishing. Brian lives in Los Angeles, CA.

To discover more please go to www.gbrianbenson.com

Made in the USA
Columbia, SC
15 November 2024